Student Support Materials for
AQA AS Sociology

Unit 2

Education with
Research Methods

iz Steel

.angley

Published by Collins Education
An imprint of HarperCollins Publishers
77-85 Fulham Palace Road
Hammersmith
London
W6 8JB

Browse the complete Collins Education catalogue at
www.collinseducation.com

10 9 8 7 6 5 4 3 2

ISBN 978-0-00-741832-9

Martin Holborn and Liz Steel assert their moral rights to be identified as the authors of this work.

British Library Cataloguing in Publication Data.

A catalogue record for this publication is available from the British Library.

Commissioned by Charlie Evans and Andrew Campbell

Project editor: Sarah Vittachi

Design and typesetting by Hedgehog Publishing Limited

Cover Design by Angela English

Production by Simon Moore

Printed and bound in China

Indexed by Indexing Specialists (UK) Ltd

Acknowledgements

Every effort has been made to contact the holders of copyright material, but if any have been inadvertently overlooked the publishers will be pleased to make the necessary arrangements at the first opportunity.

p4, source: Office for National Statistics; p12, source: Office for National Statistics; p20, source: Office for National Statistics; p28, source: Office for National Statistics; p39, Table 9, source: Office for National Statistics; p43, source: Office for National Statistics; p61, Table 18, source: Home Office.

Thanks to the following students for providing answers to the questions:

Ruby Barwood, Collette Blackman, Lauren Foley, Vicki Gill, Jessica Gowers, Fran Guratsky, Rachel Hewitt, Ella Keating, Charlotte Ross, Eric Wedge-Bull.

Functionalist perspectives

Introduction to the education system

The growth of state education

In the UK, free compulsory state education started in 1870, although since 1833 the state had made some contribution to funding education.

- In 1880 state education was made compulsory up to the age of 10.
- By 1918 children had to stay at school until the age of 14, and in 1972 the school leaving age was raised to 16.
- By 2005 more than three-quarters of all 16- to 18-year-olds were taking part in some form of education and training, and in 2007 it was announced that education and training would be made compulsory up to age 18.
- Higher education has also expanded rapidly, so that almost 40% of school leavers now go on to study at that level.

A variety of sociological perspectives have examined the role of education in society and discussed the reasons for the expansion of state education.

The functionalist perspective

Functionalists see society as an interrelated whole. To functionalists every institution in society performs one or more important **functions** or jobs and they assume that this helps society to run smoothly like a well-oiled machine. Functionalist theories of education therefore look for the positive benefits and functions that education performs for all societies.

Durkheim – education and social solidarity

Émile Durkheim (1925) saw the main role of education as the transmission of the **norms** and **values** of society. Education helps to unite all individuals within society, creating a sense of belonging and commitment to that society, or what Durkheim called **social solidarity**. By the teaching of history, individuals learn about their society and develop a sense of commitment to it.

Durkheim saw schools as societies in miniature in which individuals learn to interact with others and follow a fixed set of rules. This provides preparation for later life when individuals will have to get on with others and adhere to rules in society.

Durkheim also believed that education helps to teach the specific skills necessary in an **industrial society** with specialist jobs (an advanced **division of labour**), which could not be taught by parents, who lack the specialist knowledge.

Examiners' notes

You can get a whole range of questions on **functionalism**, including 2-, 6-, 12- and 20-mark questions. 2-mark questions might ask you to explain 'what is meant' by any of the concepts in bold on these pages, so knowing the glossary terms is important.

Examiners' notes

You are unlikely to be asked specifically about one functionalist writer, but when answering both 12- and 20-mark questions it is helpful to make reference to all three of the functionalists discussed in this section to pick up maximum marks for knowledge and understanding.

Key study

Parsons: universalistic values

Talcott Parsons (1961) believed education has three main functions.

1. It is a bridge between the family and wider society.
2. It socializes children into the basic values of society.
3. It selects people for their future roles in society.

Before attending school, children are socialized within the family where **particularistic standards** are used; that is, children are treated as particular individuals. In society as a whole, however, **universalistic standards** are usually used, in which people are judged according to standards that apply equally to everybody.

In families, **status** is fixed by birth; this is **ascribed status**. However, in society as a whole, status is based on **merit** (for example, people compete to get jobs) and status is therefore achieved.

Parsons believed that education makes the transition from family to society as a whole possible by getting people used to universalistic values and **achieved status**.

Education socializes individuals into the major values of society, the belief in **individual achievement** and in the value of **equality of opportunity**. The exam system encourages these values because it judges people fairly and motivates them to be successful.

Education also assesses students' abilities so that they can be matched to suitable jobs, allowing them to make a major contribution to society.

Davis and Moore – education and role allocation

Davis and Moore (1945) viewed education as a means of **role allocation**. Education sifts and sorts people according to their abilities so that the most able gain high qualifications and can progress to doing the most **functionally important jobs** in society. The most important jobs are more highly rewarded, thereby motivating the talented to work hard to achieve those positions. In this way, education helps to ensure that competent people fulfil the important roles in society and are motivated to work hard. Davis and Moore saw education as **meritocratic**; that is, people are judged according to their ability and effort, not according to who they are.

Criticisms of functionalism

The main criticisms of functionalism are summarized in **table 1**.

Functionalist view	Criticism
Education benefits society as a whole	**Marxists** argue that education benefits the ruling **class** (see page 6), while feminists see it as benefiting men (see page 24)
Education promotes the norms and values of society as a whole (Durkheim, Parsons)	Marxists see education as promoting the values of powerful groups. Hargreaves (1982) believes education promotes **competition** and **individualism** rather than shared values
Education promotes social solidarity (Durkheim)	Education can be divisive because of a **hierarchy** of schools and universities, which can separate **social classes**
Educational achievement is based on merit	A great deal of research shows that class, gender and ethnicity influence achievement
Education selects the most appropriate people to do particular jobs (Davis and Moore)	Other factors apart from qualifications influence the **labour market** (e.g. social contacts – who you know)

Table 1
Criticisms of functionalism

Examiners' notes

The functionalist theories can be compared and contrasted with other theories such as Marxism or **feminism**, especially in 20-mark questions, in order to gain evaluation and analysis marks.

Essential notes

There has been an immense amount of research on whether society really is meritocratic, and most of it has concluded that meritocracy is a myth. For example, your social class background seems to influence both the qualifications and the jobs that you get independently of your ability or achievements in education.

Marxist perspectives

Introduction to Marxism

According to Karl Marx (1818–1883) and Frederick Engels (1820–1895) **power** in society largely stemmed from wealth. In particular, those who owned the **means of production** (the things needed to produce other things such as land, **capital**, machinery and labour power) formed a powerful **ruling class**. They were able to exploit the **subject class** (those who did not own the means of production and therefore had to work for the ruling class).

Economic systems

According to Marx, society passed through several eras in which different economic systems or **modes of production** were dominant. In each of these there was a different ruling class and subject class. In the latest stage, **capitalist society**, the ruling class were wealthy factory owners (the **bourgeoisie**) and the subject class were the working-class employees (the proletariat). In **capitalism** the proletariat was exploited by the bourgeoisie because they were not paid the full value of the work that they did and the bourgeoisie kept some **surplus value** or profit.

The economic base and superstructure

The power of the bourgeoisie derived from their ownership of the means of production. The means of production forms the **economic base** or **infrastructure** of society. Because they controlled the economic base, the bourgeoisie were able to control the other, non-economic, institutions of society (which make up the **superstructure**), such as the media, government, religion, the family and education.

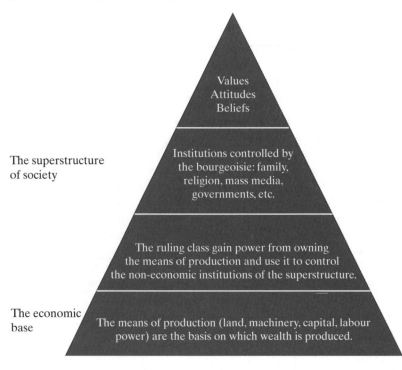

The superstructure of society

Values
Attitudes
Beliefs

Institutions controlled by the bourgeoisie: family, religion, mass media, governments, etc.

The ruling class gain power from owning the means of production and use it to control the non-economic institutions of the superstructure.

The economic base

The means of production (land, machinery, capital, labour power) are the basis on which wealth is produced.

Fig 1
A Marxist model of society

Key study

Bowles and Gintis: Capitalist schooling

Bowles and Gintis (1976) argue that education is controlled by capitalists and serves their interests. There is a close relationship between schooling and work, because schooling is used to prepare children for working in capitalist businesses. The **correspondence principle** states that education corresponds to employment.

The hidden curriculum

Capitalism requires a hard-working, obedient workforce that will not challenge the management. Bowles and Gintis believe that education prepares such a workforce through the **hidden curriculum**. This works in the following ways:

- Conformist pupils are awarded higher grades than those who challenge authority or think creatively.
- Schools teach acceptance of hierarchy, since teachers give the orders and pupils obey.
- Pupils are motivated by the **external rewards** of exam success just as workers are motivated by wages.
- Both work and education are **fragmented**, or broken into small pieces, so that workers and pupils have little overall understanding of production or society. This keeps them divided.

Bowles and Gintis see the idea of **meritocracy** as a myth and, in reality, class background as determining how well a person does. However, because people believe that the education system is meritocratic, this **legitimates** the system, making it seem fair.

Criticisms of Marxism

Marxism in general, and Bowles and Gintis in particular, have been criticized in a number of ways.

Marxist view	Criticism
Education corresponds to work	Brown et al. (1997) believe that much work now requires teamwork rather than obedience
Education creates obedient and uncritical workers	Reynolds (1984) believes that some education encourages critical thinking (e.g. sociology) Some neo-Marxists such as Willis believe that the hidden curriculum is not always accepted
Education is controlled by capitalists	Elected local education authorities and teachers have some independence and do not have to follow the wishes of capitalists
Education only benefits the ruling class	Functionalists believe that education benefits society as a whole, while feminists believe that it benefits men rather than the ruling class
Evidence supports the Marxist theory (Bowles and Gintis)	The research by Bowles and Gintis is dated, USA-focused and may not apply to today

Examiners' notes

This is a vital study, which is useful for answering any 12- or 20-mark answers about the Marxist view of the role of education in society.

Examiners' notes

You could well be given a 20-mark question asking you to describe and evaluate the Marxist and Marxist-feminist perspective. In this case, make sure you bring in neo-Marxism and Marxist feminism as well, to get into the top mark band for skills of interpretation, application, analysis and evaluation.

Essential notes

Neo-Marxist views are examined in the next section and provide partial support for Bowles and Gintis, but also offer a more sophisticated and developed viewpoint.

Table 2
Criticisms of Marxism

Examiners' notes

Alternative perspectives, which are developed in much more detail in other sections will allow you to add substance to many of these criticisms. To support Marxism you can point out that there is a good deal of research, which suggests that education is not meritocratic but influenced by social class.

Neo-Marxist perspectives

Neo-Marxism and education

Neo-Marxism is a term used to describe new versions of Marxism. They are new (neo) because they disagree in some way with the original writings of Karl Marx, while still being strongly influenced by them.

Giroux – Neo-Marxism, struggle and relative autonomy

An example of neo-Marxism applied to education is the work of Henry Giroux (1984). He disagrees with the conventional Marxist approach of Bowles and Gintis (see previous pages) in three ways.

1. Working-class pupils do not passively accept everything they are taught, but actively shape their own education and sometimes resist the discipline imposed on them by school.
2. Schools are **sites of ideological struggle** for different classes, ethnic, religious and cultural groups. Capitalists have more power than any other single group but they do not have all the power.
3. The education system possesses **relative autonomy** from the economic base; that is, it has some independence and is not always shaped by the needs of the capitalist economy.

Key study
Willis: Learning to labour

The most influential neo-Marxist study of education is an **ethnographic study** of a group of boys (or 'lads') in a Midlands **comprehensive school** in the 1970s. Paul Willis (1977) conducted the study using **interviews**, **observation** and **participant observation** in the school.

- The 'lads' saw themselves as superior to staff and other pupils.
- They were not interested in getting academic qualifications.
- They aimed to do as little work as possible while entertaining themselves through bad behaviour.
- They were unhappy at being treated as children and identified more with the adult world.
- They formed a **counterculture**, which was **sexist** (looking down on women) and **racist** (looking down on ethnic minorities). They valued traditional **working-class masculinity**, which emphasized toughness and despised weakness.
- Physical, **manual labour** was seen as more valuable than 'pen-pushing'.

Shop-floor culture and the counter-school culture

Willis followed the lads into their first jobs, often in factories. He found a **shop-floor culture** similar to the **counter-school culture**, which:

- was racist and sexist
- had little respect for authority.

Workers did as little work as possible and tried to enjoy themselves through, 'having a laff'. They developed ways of coping with boring work over which they had little control. Paul Willis argues that to some extent the lads saw through the capitalist system, perceiving that they had little chance of progressing through hard work in education to well-paid or high status jobs.

However, he also saw that their actions led them into jobs where they were exploited by the ruling class.

Examiners' notes

Do not forget to criticize the study for its small unrepresentative sample and for being dated if you use it in 12- or 20-mark answers.

Comparison and evaluation of Marxism and neo-Marxism

Table 3 compares and evaluates the work of the most influential Marxists, Bowles and Gintis and the most influential neo-Marxist, Paul Willis.

Marxism – Bowles and Gintis	Neo-Marxism – Paul Willis
Key concepts	
The correspondence principle, the hidden curriculum, the myth of meritocracy	Counter-school culture, shop-floor culture, 'having a laff'
Relationship between capitalism and education	
Capitalism directly shapes the content of education and controls the behaviour of pupils	Capitalism shapes society as a whole but groups within education form their own subcultures
View of pupil behaviour	
Pupils conform within school	Some pupils actively rebel against school
Relationship between school and work	
Schools create passive, obedient workers who will be easily exploited	Schools creates poorly behaved workers, but workers who do not rebel against the capitalist system as a whole
Main strengths	
Analyses the overall relationship between education and capitalist society	Based on detailed ethnographic research. Shows a subtle understanding of behaviour in schools. Does not assume that most pupils conform
Main weaknesses	
Based on limited evidence. Exaggerates the control of capitalists over education. Doesn't examine the positive benefits of education or explore gender inequalities within education	Dated, and based on a very small sample. Oversimplifies school subcultures into two types: pro- and anti-school. Relies too much on Willis' own interpretation of the lads' behaviour

Examiners' notes

This table is useful for providing high-level analysis, necessary for the top mark band in longer questions.

Table 3
Comparison and evaluation of Bowles and Gintis, and Willis

Social democratic and New Right perspectives

Introduction

Functionalist, Marxist and neo-Marxist perspectives are all based on specific sociological theories, but some views of the relationship between education and society are based more on political **ideologies** and associated social policies relating to the education system. Two such approaches are the **social democratic** and **New Right** perspectives. Social democratic perspectives are more **left wing** (in favour of greater equality and greater state intervention in the economy) and the New Right are more **right wing** (in favour of competition and **free markets**).

Social democratic perspectives on education

From this perspective, governments should play a major role in providing welfare through the **state** for its citizens in order to promote the well-being of members of society. Society produces inequality of **income** and wealth, which creates **inequality of opportunity**. Those from advantaged backgrounds tend to do better in the education system.

The role of the state should be to make opportunity more equal and society more **meritocratic**. In a meritocracy, success and failure in education and in the labour market are based on effort and ability.

Social democratic perspectives influenced Labour governments of the 1960s and 70s. They were opposed to the **tripartite** system in which pupils went to one of three types of school:

- **grammar schools**, which provided an academic education for those who had passed the 11+ exam
- **secondary modern schools**, which provided a more vocational education
- **technical schools**, for those with technical ability.

Grammar schools were **selective**, taking only higher-ability pupils. Social democrats believe this system was divisive because most pupils in grammar schools were from **middle-class** backgrounds, whereas most in secondary modern schools were from **working-class** backgrounds.

Social democratic policies

The Labour governments of the 1960s and 70s partly replaced the tripartite educational system with comprehensive schools which all pupils attended. The intention was to:

- get rid of class divisions between different types of schools
- create more equal opportunities
- encourage economic growth by ensuring that talent was not wasted through sending talented pupils to secondary modern schools where they would not develop their skills fully.

The Labour government also worked to reduce inequality in society through taxation and welfare policies in which the rich were more heavily taxed than others (**progressive taxation**), and welfare was provided to the less well-off so that they did not live in **poverty**.

New Right perspectives on education

The New Right (also sometimes called **neo-liberals** or **market liberals**) are opposed to the views of social democrats.

The New Right believe:
- **Private enterprise**, based on competition between businesses, is the most efficient system for running any service.
- Services provided by the state tend to be inefficient. This is because the producers have no incentive to work hard since, unlike business, there is no competition.
- There are no customers paying for the service, meaning that state education is unresponsive to its customers.
- Competition is essential to raising standards, which is vital if the UK is to produce the highly educated adults who are necessary to compete in the global economy.
- The main focus of education should be on training the workforce.
- Training the workforce requires a new emphasis on **vocational** education.

New Right policies
The New Right perspective on education influenced the policies of the Conservative governments of Margaret Thatcher and John Major from 1979 to 1997. The main features of these policies were:
- They introduced market forces and competition between educational institutions.
- Schools competed for pupils, and unpopular schools lost money.
- Greater **choice** was introduced with new types of schools such as **grant-maintained schools** funded directly by the government.
- The **National Curriculum**, **league tables**, regular inspections and frequent testing were all designed to drive up standards in order to make the UK more economically competitive.

Social democratic and New Right perspectives compared
Table 4 outlines the main similarities and differences, and strengths and weaknesses of these perspectives.

Social democratic perspective	New Right perspective
Aim of education	
To promote greater equality, reduce class divisions and promote economic growth. To provide equality of opportunity	To raise standards and promote economic growth. To train the workforce needed by business
Policies supported	
Comprehensive schools, growing welfare state, higher income tax for the rich	Competition and parental choice in education, reduced state expenditure
Governments influenced	
Labour governments of 1960s and 70s	Conservative governments of 1979–97
Ideology	
Left wing, seeing state and redistribution of wealth as desirable	Right wing, seeing a small state and private enterprise as desirable

Essential notes

The New Right believe that raising standards will promote economic growth, but this is best achieved through competition rather than spending more government money.

Examiners' notes

If you are asked about education and the economy, discuss the New Right argument that too much spending on education will lead to higher taxes, which will prevent economic growth.

Examiners' notes

If you are asked a 20-mark question about the New Right you can expand on the material here by using the discussion of policies found on pages 38–39.

Examiners' notes

Do not forget that in any question asking you to evaluate a theory, including Marxism and functionalism, these perspectives can be brought in to provide contrast and criticism.

Table 4
Social democratic and New Right perspectives compared

Examiners' notes

You will not need to provide definitions of class for shorter answers, but a short definition can be helpful at the start of 20- and sometimes 12-mark questions to pick up knowledge and understanding marks.

Social class: introduction

Introduction

Differential educational achievement refers to differences in the level of educational qualification achieved by social groups.

Social classes can be defined in a number of ways, but all definitions are based on the idea that groups in society can be divided according to their economic circumstances. For example, income, wealth and occupation are frequently seen as the most important factors distinguishing social classes.

On this basis, three main classes can be distinguished:

1. The **upper class**, who own significant amounts of wealth; for example, land, property, businesses or shares.
2. The **middle class**, who have **non-manual** jobs (that is, their jobs primarily involve mental rather than physical labour) with relatively high pay and job security. They usually have higher-level qualifications.
3. The **working class**, who have **manual jobs** (their jobs primarily involve physical labour). They do not usually have higher-level qualifications and on average have lower pay and less job security than the middle class.

Evidence of class inequality in differential achievement

Class inequalities in differential achievement are usually measured through a comparison of classes based on **occupational groups**.

Essential notes

Despite numerous policies that have attempted to narrow the gap in the achievement of different classes in the education system, there is little overall evidence of any significant change. This might suggest that factors outside the education system are playing a major role, and that the gap is unlikely to decline much without a reduction in inequality in society as a whole.

A wide range of data shows continuing and significant inequalities in educational achievement by social class. In 2003, less than 40% of children from working-class backgrounds achieved five or more GCSEs at grades A*–C, whereas more than 65% of children from middle-class backgrounds achieved this level. This represents a gap of 24 percentage points between the classes.

There are also differences in participation rates in post-compulsory education. In 2005, 86% of children from the highest class remained in full-time education after 16, compared with 62% of those from the lowest class.

The differences are even greater in higher education. Government figures show that, in 2005, 59% of 19-year-olds from the highest class were in higher education, compared with 19% of those from the lowest class. Furthermore, between 2003 and 2005, participation by the highest class went up seven percentage points, whereas participation from the lowest class went up just five percentage points.

The evidence therefore shows a large and persistent gap between the educational attainment of higher and lower classes.

A variety of theories have been used to explain inequalities in achievements:

- Some have emphasized **cultural factors**, while others have emphasized **material factors** (that is, differences in income and resources).

- Some have emphasized factors in the education system itself, whereas others have emphasized factors outside the education system.

Class subcultures and educational achievement

A number of theories emphasizing factors outside the education system have blamed the underachievement of the working class in education on the inadequacy of working-class culture, particularly inside working-class homes. These theories are known as **cultural deprivation** theories (the working class are deprived of the **culture** necessary for educational success).

Early research by sociologists such as David Lockwood (1966) claimed to identify distinctive **subcultures** associated with the middle class and the working class.

	Working class	Middle class
Time orientation:	**Present-time orientation** – live life in the moment rather than worrying about the future	**Future-time orientation** – think ahead rather than living in the moment
Attitude to gratification:	Seek **immediate gratification** – enjoy yourself now (e.g. spending your wage packet as soon as you are paid)	**Deferred gratification** – put off pleasure now in order to achieve greater pleasure in the future (e.g. saving for a deposit on a house)
Collectivism versus individualism:	Success achieved through collective action (e.g. a union going on strike)	Success achieved through individual action (e.g. studying or working hard)
Attitudes to luck:	Your chances in life are based on luck or fate (**fatalism**)	Your chances in life are based on ability and hard work: you make your own luck

It is debatable how far these **class subcultures** still exist today, but some sociologists have argued that there are still differences in social class subcultures and these might affect educational achievement.

- Barry Sugarman (1970) argues that the **present-time orientation** and inability to defer gratification of the working class makes them unlikely to sacrifice immediate income in order to stay on in education to gain higher wages and a better job in the longterm.
- In addition, the fatalism of the working class means they generally do not believe that they can improve their prospects through their own hard work.
- The **collectivist** approach makes them less likely to pursue individual success through the education system.

Examiners' notes

It is quite common to get 20-mark questions asking you to evaluate whether cultural or material factors are more important, or alternatively whether factors inside or outside the education system are most important. Make sure you know which categories each approach comes into.

Table 5
Social class subcultures

Examiners' notes

You will not need to go through all these differences in detail, but you should use the main concepts and outline the differences if you need to discuss cultural factors that affect educational achievement.

This topic continues on the next two pages

Examiners' notes

This is a useful example of a longitudinal study to refer to in answers about research methods applied to education.

Key study
Douglas: Cultural deprivation

In an influential **longitudinal study**, J.W.B. Douglas (1964, 1970) followed the careers of over 5000 children through the education system. Douglas found that working-class parents showed less interest in their children's education than middle-class parents. For example, working-class parents:

- visited school less often to discuss their children's progress
- were less keen than the middle class for their children to stay on at school after the minimum leaving age.

Douglas also found that working-class parents gave their children less attention and stimulation during their early years. He therefore believed that differences in **primary socialization** between the social classes explained the relative educational failure of the working class.

More recent research by Feinstein (2003) used data from the National Child Development Study to examine the effects of cultural and other factors in shaping educational achievement. Feinstein found:

- Financial deprivation (having poorer parents) had some effect on achievement.
- Cultural deprivation was much more important, and the extent to which parents encouraged and supported their children was the crucial factor in determining how well they did.

Evaluation of cultural deprivation theory

Cultural deprivation theory has been heavily criticized. Blackstone and Mortimore (1994), for example, argue that:

- Research has not measured parental interest in education adequately. Teachers' assessments have often been used and these may not reflect the real level of interest of parents.
- Working-class parents may feel less able to visit school because they feel uncomfortable interacting with middle-class teachers.
- Schools with more middle-class children tend to have more organized systems of parent–school contacts.

Examiners' notes

Cultural deprivation theory has been heavily criticized because it seems to blame the working class for a system which disadvantages them. Make sure that you point out the weaknesses of the theory in all 20-mark answers, and include some evaluation in 12-mark answers.

Key study
Basil Bernstein: Speech patterns

Bernstein (1972) believes that a particular aspect of culture – speech – shapes educational achievement. He distinguishes two types of speech patterns:

- **Restricted codes** – are a type of shorthand speech in which meanings are not made fully explicit. They are characterized by short, simple and often unfinished sentences. This type of speech code is more typical of the working class, who are more likely than the middle class to communicate verbally in their jobs and less likely to need to write reports.

- **Elaborated codes** – are types of speech in which the meanings are filled in and made explicit; sentences tend to be longer and more complex. These are more likely to be used in middle-class jobs where there is a greater requirement to write reports and produce **documents**.

In education, elaborated codes are necessary for exam success in many subjects, and as teachers are themselves middle class they are more likely to use elaborated codes. Being socialized in households that largely use restricted codes holds back the working class in the education system, making it more difficult for them to achieve academic success.

Bernstein, however, has been criticized by Gaine and George (1999). They argue that:

- Bernstein oversimplifies the differences between middle- and working-class speech patterns.
- Many other factors apart from speech affect educational attainment.
- Class differences in speech patterns have declined since Bernstein did his research.

Compensatory education

Although cultural deprivation theory has been heavily criticized, it has influenced a range of educational policies. These policies have led to the idea of positive discrimination in the form of **compensatory education** – the working class are given extra help in the education system to compensate for the inadequacy of their socialization. In recent decades, a variety of schemes have provided extra help for the working class. These range from **Education Action Zones** in the 1970s, to **Sure Start**, which since 1998 has provided additional pre-school education to try to compensate for any lack of educational stimulation from parents.

Critics such as Whitty (2002) believe that all these schemes place blame for failure on the child and her or his background and ignore the effects of inequality in society as a whole. Many schemes have lacked resources and have failed to tackle the poverty that is the underlying cause of educational inequality.

Examiners' notes

This could feature in a 2-mark or 6-mark question. It can also be useful for developing the evaluation of cultural deprivation, since policies based upon the theory have had limited effectiveness.

Social class: Cultural and material factors

Bourdieu: Capital and educational achievement

Some sociologists accept that culture can play a part in educational achievement, not because the working class lack an adequate culture but because the education system is essentially fixed in favour of people with upper- or middle-class backgrounds.

Pierre Bourdieu (1984) believes that your parents' possession (or lack) of one of four different types of capital can affect your achievement in the education system.

Table 6
Bourdieu: types of capital and education

Definition	Example	Role in education
Economic capital		
Ownership of wealth	Owning valuable houses, shares, having an income	Paying for private education or additional tuition
Cultural capital		
Possession of educational qualifications, knowledge of arts and literature, and lifestyles, which are valued in society	Degree-level qualification or higher, educational holidays, knowledge of classic art and literature	Knowledge and experience to help children with school work. Educationally stimulating home environment – children become familiar with knowledge that is valued at school
Social capital		
Possession of valuable social contacts	Knowing teachers, head-teachers, professors socially	May help with admission to best educational institutions or finding expert help
Symbolic capital		
Possession of status	Having an image of respectability	Could help with admission to **private** or **selective schools**

All these types of capital can help in education and all reflect class inequalities in society. However, **cultural capital** is particularly useful. The education system is biased towards the culture of higher social classes. Students from these classes therefore have an advantage because they have been socialized into the **dominant culture**.

Essential notes

Bourdieu's ideas have been very influential. He was influenced by Marxist thinking (the dominant culture in society is reflected in the school **curriculum** and this helps those from higher or middle-class backgrounds), but he did not only discuss economic factors.

Examiners' notes

This theory is essential in questions on class and differential achievement, as it helps to link factors inside and outside school. It can also be used to develop the Marxist theory in theory questions.

Key study

Stephen Ball et al.: Cultural capital and educational choice

Bourdieu's theory was supported in a study of parental choice in education by Ball and colleagues (2000). They looked at the process of choosing a secondary school and found that middle-class parents had a significant advantage over working-class parents.

- Middle-class parents have the knowledge and contacts to play the system to give their children the best chance of getting into the most successful schools (cultural and social capital).
- Working-class parents lacked the money to pay for transport to send their children to better but more distant schools, or to move into the **catchment area** of a successful school.

- Working-class parents were just as keen for their children to do well in education but they lacked the cultural capital and **material resources** to ensure success.

Reay et al.: Social class and higher education

A study by Reay et al. found that cultural differences between classes affected choice of university. According to Bourdieu, each class has its own **habitus** (dispositions, tastes and lifestyle) and only feel comfortable in their own habitus.

Elite universities such as Oxford or Cambridge tend to have an upper-class habitus, which meant that sixth-form students from working-class schools were unlikely to apply.

Material factors and educational achievement

Despite the importance attached to culture by the above studies, they all see class inequalities based on material factors of wealth and income as the basis for the class divisions, which produce different cultures.

A number of researchers believe that material inequality directly causes class differences in educational achievement.

Smith and Noble: Material factors in schooling

Smith and Noble (1995) identify the following ways in which having more money gives advantages to middle-class and upper-class pupils in the schooling system.

1. Having money makes it possible for parents to provide more books and educational toys, healthier diets, space to study in the home, computer facilities, private tuition and educational travel abroad.
2. Schools increasingly charge for trips, material and equipment and extra tuition in subjects like music. This puts the children of wealthy parents at an advantage.
3. Schools in more affluent areas tend to be more successful and attract more pupils; this results in their getting more funding.

Material factors and higher education

Research by Reay et al. (2005) into higher education found that material factors, as well as cultural factors, were important.

- More than a quarter of children at private schools received extra private tuition to help them get into the best universities.
- Working-class students were more likely to apply to local universities than middle-class students in order to save money on travel. This gave them less opportunity to go to the most prestigious universities.
- Students from poorer backgrounds often had to work part-time to fund their studies, making it more difficult for them to get higher-class degrees.

Callender and Jackson (2004) used survey research to examine the effects of the introduction of tuition fees into higher education, and the replacement of most grants with loans. They found that potential applicants from poorer backgrounds were most afraid of leaving university with high debt and therefore more likely to decide not to go to university.

Examiners' notes

This study is also important in answering questions on policies because it shows how the market in education introduced by the New Right can be manipulated to benefit those from higher classes.

Examiners' notes

In 12-mark questions you need to develop three or four explanations of material inequality and include some evaluation, while in 20-mark questions it will be important to contrast this type of explanation with cultural explanations and factors inside the education system.

Examiners' notes

Access to higher education is a topic of great contemporary relevance, given increases in student fees, so it is likely to impress the examiner if you can show knowledge of recent changes and apply it to a question.

Examiners' notes

You only need to discuss this background if asked specifically about the interactionist perspective.

Social class: Factors within education

The interactionist perspective

Cultural deprivation and material explanations of differential educational achievement by social class both see factors outside the education system as responsible for class differences. The interactionist perspective, however, focuses on processes within schools and other educational institutions to explain differential achievement.

While interacting with others, people interpret and attach meanings to the behaviour of those around them. This affects people's image of themselves (**self-concept**), and self-concept in turn shapes behaviour. For example, if pupils are labelled as **deviants** or troublemakers their behaviour will tend to be seen as a deliberate attempt to cause trouble. The reaction of teachers will lead to the pupils also seeing themselves as deviants, and because of this they will tend to act in more deviant ways.

Labelling

- According to the interactionist perspective, teachers may **label** pupils, or classify them into different types, and then act towards them on the basis of this classification.
- Hargreaves, Hester and Mellor (1975) found that factors such as a pupil's appearance, how they respond to discipline, how likeable they are and their personality, as well as whether they are deviant, leads to teachers attaching labels to them as 'good' or 'bad' pupils.
- Once given a label, teachers tend to interpret behaviour in terms of that label, and pupils tend to live up to the label.
- This results in a **self-fulfilling-prophecy,** in which the label results in the behaviour predicted by the teacher.
  1. Teacher forms impression of pupil
  2. Pupil labelled as a troublemaker and teacher interprets behaviour as deviant
  3. Pupil becomes aware of teacher's label
  4. Pupil self-concept starts to change
  5. Pupil starts living up to label
  6. Initial label confirmed by behaviour; stronger labelling and more deviant behaviour occurs

Social class and labelling

Many interactionists claim that social class background affects the way that teachers label pupils. Middle-class pupils fit the teacher's **stereotype** of the **ideal pupil** better than working-class pupils, and therefore working-class pupils are more likely to be labelled as deviant or lazy.

Labelling can lead to pupils being placed in different ability groupings within school. Lower-class pupils may be more likely to be placed in lower **sets**, **bands** or **streams**. These lower groupings are likely to be seen as less able and as more likely to be disruptive. This can lead to the formation of pupil **subcultures**, with lower streams or sets more likely to form anti-

Examiners' notes

This material is important for questions about processes within schools generally, not just questions on class and differential achievement.

school subcultures. Among these pupils, academic work is not valued and **peer groups** encourage deviant behaviour and discourage hard work.

Key study
Mac an Ghaill: Labelling and peer groups

Máirtin Mac an Ghaill (1994) studied working-class students in a Midlands comprehensive school. The school had divided pupils into three sets and, as a result, three distinct, male, working-class peer groups developed:

- 'Macho lads' – academic failures who became hostile to the school and were usually from less skilled working-class backgrounds.
- 'Academic achievers' – academic 'successes', usually from more skilled working-class backgrounds, they tried hard at school.
- 'New enterprisers' – had a positive attitude to school and saw the vocational **curriculum** as a route to career success.

Evaluation of interactionist approaches

Interactionist studies of education have certain advantages over other approaches:

- They are often based on detailed empirical evidence.
- They show that factors operating within school can have a significant impact on educational achievement.

However, they have been criticized as follows:

- They fail to explain where wider class inequalities come from.
- They ignore factors outside the school such as cultural and material factors, which may also affect achievement.
- They use simplified models of pupil subcultures and do not identify the full range of responses to school.
- Labelling theory sometimes sounds **deterministic**. Success and failure is entirely determined by the attitudes of teachers, giving pupils little apparent control over their own success.
- Not all pupils live up to labelling by teachers. A study by Margaret Fuller (1984) found that a group of black working-class girls who were labelled as likely failures responded by working harder to achieve success.

Essential notes

This study demonstrates how class interacts with gender in shaping achievement.

Examiners' notes

It is very important to emphasize that all the main types of inequality – class, gender and ethnicity – act together in shaping differential educational achievement. You can get analysis and evaluation marks for pointing this out, and then further marks if you back it up with reference to specific studies.

Essential notes

Whatever the merits of these particular studies and the interactionist approach, there is little doubt that the nature of schools themselves plays some part in determining educational achievement. For example, some schools with a predominantly working-class intake do better than other schools with similar pupils. Overall, though, it is very difficult for the educational system to compensate for the inequalities in society as a whole.

Examiners' notes

Look out for 2-mark questions asking you to define terms like ethnicity.

Ethnicity and educational achievement

Ethnicity

- **Ethnic groups** are groups within a population regarded by themselves or others as culturally distinctive; they usually see themselves as having a common origin. Ethnicity may be linked to religion, nationality and other aspects of culture such as language and lifestyle.
- Largely as a result of **migration**, the UK has a number of distinctive ethnic groups. The largest minority ethnic groups in the UK are those of South Asian or African-Caribbean origin. The Irish and Chinese can also be regarded as minority ethnic groups.
- There are significant differences in educational achievement between ethnic groups, although the achievement gap between some ethnic groups has been narrowing.
- There are also differences in achievement between males and females within ethnic groups.

Ethnic differences in achievement

One way of measuring educational achievement is by looking at the proportion of pupils gaining five or more GCSEs at grades A*–C. In 2004:

- Chinese pupils had the highest proportion achieving this level (79% of girls and 70% of boys)
- followed by Indian pupils (72% of girls and 62% of boys)
- lowest levels of attainment were among black African-Caribbean pupils, particularly boys (44% of girls and just 27% of boys).

Another measure is to look at the highest qualification attained. In 2004, 31% of Chinese, 25% of Indians, 17% of white British people and 13% of black African-Caribbean people had degrees.

Changes over time

Over the past 20 years, minority ethnic groups have been gaining ground on white British people in the education system.

- In 1992, white British pupils were more than twice as likely as Bangladeshis to achieve five or more GCSEs at grades A*–C, but by 2006 there was only one percentage point difference between them.
- By 2001–2, all minority ethnic groups had higher participation rates in higher education than white British people in England.
- Nevertheless, minority ethnic groups are still less likely to go to the more prestigious universities and, apart from Chinese and Indians, are less likely to attain a high-grade degree.

Social class, ethnicity and achievement

Differences in achievement are partly the result of social class differences. Most minority ethnic groups are more likely to have working-class jobs than white British people. Since class has a major impact on levels of educational achievement, this partly explains underachievement by members of some minority ethnic groups.

Essential notes

Differences in the highest qualification achieved by different groups is partly the result of historical differences in achievement and do not fully reflect more recent progress by minority ethnic groups.

Examiners' notes

Some detail on differences and changes can help you to get into top mark bands on longer questions. It is useful to analyse the causes of differential achievement by trying to identify differences between ethnic groups.

However, research by Modood (2004) found that class differences in achievement at GCSE were greatest among white British and lower among minority ethnic groups.

Modood argues that some ethnic minority pupils have higher levels of cultural capital, despite often being from a working-class background. For example, many Indians and East African Asians originate from **working-class** backgrounds even though they have **middle-class** jobs. The parents therefore may place a particularly high value on educational success and they have the knowledge and understanding of education to help their children to succeed.

Cultural factors, ethnicity and achievement

Differences in educational achievements could also be the result of cultural factors such as the educational qualifications of parents and parental knowledge of, and interest in, the education system.

> **Key study**
>
> **Strand: Ethnicity and achievement in secondary education**
>
> Strand (2007) compared the progress of Indian, African-Caribbean and white British pupils in the first four years of secondary school. Strand found that Indian children made more progress than white British children but African-Caribbean pupils fell further behind. The success of Indian pupils was due to both cultural and material factors such as:
>
> - high aspirations and dedication to homework
> - low levels of truancy and exclusion
> - good resource provision at home (such as computers or private tuition).
>
> African-Caribbean pupils were held back mainly by material factors such as:
>
> - high levels of poverty
> - living in poor accommodation
> - attending schools in deprived areas.
>
> There was no evidence, however, that African-Caribbean parents and pupils had a culture that would hold them back in education – they had high aspirations and a positive attitude to school. Overall the study found little difference in the cultural support for education between working-class white and African-Caribbean pupils, so it was difficult to explain why African-Caribbean pupils were doing less well.

Family life, masculinity and underachievement

Tony Sewell (1997) claims that factors outside school explain the low achievement of many African-Caribbean boys. He argues that:

- A high proportion of these boys are raised in lone-parent families headed by women.
- They therefore lack a positive adult male role model.
- This makes them vulnerable to peer pressure.

Examiners' notes

The interaction of class, gender and ethnicity is always useful in answers on differential achievement. Research suggests that class is the most important factor, so mention that class differences are bound to have an effect on ethnic differences in achievement. Class may affect some ethnic groups more than others, suggesting that the relationship is quite complex.

Examiners' notes

You always need to back up claims in this area with evidence from studies such as this. Otherwise you risk your answer seeming more like stereotypical comments about ethnic groups than good sociology.

☞ **This topic continues on the next two pages**

- They are more likely to be drawn into gangs, which emphasize macho masculinity.
- Gang culture compensates for a sense of rejection by fathers and the experience of **racism** in society and in school.
- Although most African-Caribbean boys try hard to succeed in school, a significant minority of about a quarter make little effort and form an anti-school culture or reject school in favour of street culture.

Sewell's arguments have been criticized by those who believe that he is blaming black culture for educational failure, when the real cause lies in racism within the education system, or society as a whole.

Racism and educational underachievement

- Racism can be defined as negative beliefs or discriminatory behaviour directed at individuals or groups as a result of their 'race' or ethnicity.
- **Institutional racism** has been defined as 'the collective failure of an organization to provide an appropriate and professional service to people because of their colour, culture, or ethnic origin' (MacPherson, 1999).

A number of sociologists believe that the educational underachievement of some ethnic minorities, particularly African-Caribbean boys, is a result of racism, especially institutional racism.

This is reflected in school exclusion figures. In 2003/4, 41 black African-Caribbean pupils per 10 000 were excluded from school, compared with 14 per 10 000 among whites and two or less among Indians and Chinese pupils.

African-Caribbean boys are particularly likely to be placed in lower sets.

Bernard Coard (1971) claimed that there was systematic racism in British education, with teachers having low expectations of black pupils, a curriculum that ignored black history and culture, and schools that tolerated casual racism in the playground.

These views are partly supported by some studies:

Wright: Racism in primary schools

- Cecile Wright (1992) conducted an ethnographic study of four multi-racial primary schools using observation and interviews with teachers. She found significant evidence of discrimination by teachers.
- Asian girls got less attention from teachers than other pupils, and their customs and traditions were sometimes met with hostility.
- African-Caribbean boys got plenty of attention from teachers, but nearly all of it was negative – teachers expected them to behave badly.

Gillborn, Mirza and Youdell: Rationing education

Gillborn, Mirza and Youdell (2000) used documentary evidence about local education authorities, lesson observation and interviews with pupils and teachers in two London comprehensive schools.

They found evidence that some local authorities were particularly poor at educating ethnic minorities.

Within schools, they found a system of **educational triage**, in which education was rationed. Extra help was directed to pupils who were borderline for gaining five GCSEs at grades A*–C. Most black pupils were seen as having little chance of achieving this and so were not given extra help. Compared with white peers with similar levels of achievement, black pupils were placed in lower sets and entered for lower-tier exams.

There was also evidence of a system of racialized expectations. The behaviour of black pupils was often misinterpreted as threatening, when in reality it reflected a desire to take an active part in lessons and to succeed.

They conclude that unintentional racism based on misinterpretations holds back black pupils.

Racism and the curriculum
Some sociologists argue that the curriculum neglects both ethnic minority culture and topics of specific interest to ethnic minorities. For example, geography and history tend to emphasize the positive benefits of British colonialism rather than the negative effects on the former colonies.

Tikly et al. (2006) studied 30 comprehensive schools and found that a large number of African-Caribbean pupils felt that their culture was invisible in the curriculum because of a white European focus. When black history was mentioned, it tended to be in relation to slavery rather than the positive contribution of black people to history.

Conclusion
Inequality has been reduced, with most ethnic minority groups doing well in British education, but some significant problems remain, particularly for African-Caribbean boys.

The evidence suggests that factors inside and outside school combine to affect the performance of ethnic minorities in the education system.

- Unintentional racism in education probably plays some part in the **underachievement** of African-Caribbean pupils in particular.
- Some steps have been made to reduce unintentional racism, for example, through the introduction of a **multicultural curriculum.**
- Parental attitudes are probably not a factor, since research suggests parents from all ethnic groups are strongly interested in their children's education.
- Class inequality partially explains ethnic differences in achievement. It affects the educational achievements of all ethnic minorities, and has a particularly strong effect among white British, but little effect among Chinese and Indian pupils.
- Ethnicity interacts with class and gender to shape educational achievement, rather than acting independently of other social divisions.

Gender and achievement: Girls

Patterns of achievement

Historically, females have tended to achieve less well than males at higher levels in the British education system. Although girls always did better in the early years, until the early 1990s boys were more likely to gain A-level qualifications and to go on to study in higher education. Then, during the 1990s, girls overtook boys at all levels in the education system.

- In 2007, 66% of girls achieved five or more GCSEs at grades A*–C compared with 57% of boys.
- The proportion of females in the UK achieving two or more A-levels or equivalent increased from 20% in 1990 to 42% in 2006. Over the same period, the proportion of males achieving the same level increased from 18% to 33%.
- In 2006, 30% of 17-year-old males and 37% of females went on to higher education.
- Furthermore, on average, women now get better degrees than men.

Gender and subject choice

There continue to be significant differences in the choice of subjects by males and females. The National Curriculum has restricted subject choice at lower levels in the education system, but at A-level and degree level, and in vocational education, males and females still tend to choose different subjects.

At A-level:
- Males are more likely to do business studies, economics, politics, sciences (apart from biology), technical subjects and politics.
- Females are more likely to do all other subjects and for English, modern languages, psychology and sociology they are the big majority of candidates.

At degree level:
- Men are more likely to graduate in physical sciences, maths, engineering, technology, architecture, building and planning.
- Women are more likely to graduate in all other subjects and have overtaken males in medicine, dentistry and business and financial studies.

Feminist perspectives on education: Female underachievement and gendered curriculum choice

Despite the relative success of females in the education system, feminists have identified ways in which females may have been disadvantaged. Feminists generally believe that the education system is **patriarchal** or male-dominated. Although feminist perspectives may be more relevant to previous decades, some of the processes may still prevent females from achieving their full potential within education. There are also some areas where women still seem to be at a disadvantage.

- The feminist Miriam David (2008) points out that women are proportionately more likely to attend new, post-1992 universities than more prestigious institutions.

- Female disadvantage may still have an effect on subject choices, and particularly the under-representation of women in most science subjects.

Key study
Classroom behaviour

The feminist Michelle Stanworth (1983) studied A-level classes in a further education college. She found the following bias against girls:

- Teachers found it more difficult to remember the girls in their class.
- Teachers did not expect even the most able girls to go into high-status jobs.
- Pupils believed that boys received more attention than girls, and boys were more likely to join in classroom discussion and to be asked questions by the teachers.
- Girls underestimated their own ability.

Stanworth's research has been criticized by Randall (1987) for being based on interviews rather than direct observation of classroom interaction. Randall's own research failed to find the same bias against girls.

Francis: Girls and achievement

Some more recent studies by Francis (2000) do suggest that there continues to be some disadvantages for girls in the education system.

- Research in London schools found that males still dominate classrooms.
- Boys are disciplined more frequently and more harshly than girls, but this leads to girls getting less attention than boys.
- Gender divisions in subject choice are getting stronger, with fewer women taking IT and pure science degrees.

Colley: Gender inequalities in subject choice

Colley (1998) explains the continuing differences in subject choice by gender in the following way.

- Traditional definitions of masculinity and **femininity** are still widespread.
- Subjects continue to have different images; for example, computer studies, which involves working with machines rather than people and offers little opportunity for group activities, still retains a masculine image.
- Girls tend to feel comfortable with scientific and technical subjects only when taught in single-sex schools or single-sex classes.

Socialization

Norman et al. (1988) argue that **sex stereotyping** starts from a very young age. For example:
- Girls are given dolls and other toys that emphasize a caring role; this can affect career aspirations and subject choice.

Essential notes

Despite its age, this is a useful study for illustrating many of the basic points made by feminists. As the more recent research by Francis shows, classroom interaction may still be male-dominated.

Examiners' notes

These points could form the basis of an answer to a 6-mark question or could be developed further in a 12-mark question.

This topic continues on the next two pages

- Boys are more likely to be given constructional toys and other toys that help to develop scientific and mathematical skills and concepts.
- Gender stereotypes are continually reinforced through the media.

Feminist perspectives: Conclusion

Radical feminists continue to argue that society as a whole is male-dominated or patriarchal.

Liberal feminists also think that society is patriarchal to an extent, but they do accept that important changes have taken place, so that the inequality between men and women has declined.

Since females now do better than males in most aspects of the education system, there is little support for radical feminist perspectives in the evidence about changes in the education system.

Liberal feminism is on stronger ground in arguing that there are still some ways in which females lose out in the education system. Males still do better than females in some of the more prestigious subjects and are more likely to gain entry to more prestigious universities. It is also possible that there continue to be disadvantages for females, which prevent them from doing even better than they do now. **Gender roles** in society and **gender socialization** still seem to have an impact on subject choice and aspirations, although to a much lesser extent than in the past.

Reasons for improvements in girls' achievement

The performance of girls in education has improved in absolute terms – they achieve more and get higher qualifications. Also, in relative terms, they have overtaken boys. A variety of explanations have been put forward for this change.

Changes in the labour market

Opportunities for women in the labour market have greatly improved, creating more incentive for women to succeed in education.

The proportion of women of working age in employment has risen from approximately 50% in 1960 to more than 75%. There has been an expansion of **service sector** jobs, which are seen as more suitable for women, and a contraction of manual jobs and jobs in manufacturing, regarded as more suitable for men.

Francis and Skelton (2005) found that jobs with a predominantly female workforce increasingly require degree-level qualifications (for example, nursing, teaching and occupational therapy). This provides incentives for women to continue in post-compulsory education.

Changes in women's aspirations

A number of changes have affected the aspirations of women and made them more likely to aspire to high educational qualifications.

Key study
Sue Sharpe: Girls' aspirations

Sue Sharpe (1976, 1994) interviewed a sample of girls in the 1970s and a similar sample in the 1990s. She found that over this time their priorities had changed. In the 70s, love and marriage were their first priority, but by the 90s, jobs and careers were top of the list, with love and marriage seen as less important.

Examiners' notes

This is a straightforward study, which makes an important point. It is also potentially useful for discussing the use of interviews in studying education.

Francis and Skelton (2005) found that middle-class parents are increasingly concerned about the educational success of their daughters and no longer prioritize the educational achievement of sons.

Mitsos and Browne (1998) believe that the women's movement and feminism have raised the aspirations, expectations and self-esteem of women, so that they aspire to professional and managerial jobs and to achieving qualifications that will enable them to get such jobs.

Essential notes

One example of this is parents being more willing to pay for private education for their daughters than they were in the past.

Socialization for schooling

- Evidence suggests that girls are putting more effort into homework and taking education more seriously than boys.
- Research by Burns and Bracey (2001) has found that girls are better organized and more willing to draft and redraft assignments. They also found that girls tend to read more than boys. This helps them to succeed in subjects requiring the use of language.

Changes in education

Feminist research in the 1980s helped to increase awareness of possible gender bias against girls in the education system and has made educational institutions more aware of the need to provide equal opportunities for girls.

The introduction of the National Curriculum has removed any tendency for girls to be denied access to academic subjects previously only made available to boys.

- Pirie (2001) believes that the shift towards coursework has benefited girls at the expense of boys. Research suggests that boys tend to cram for exams quite effectively but are poor at organizing themselves to be successful at coursework.
- However, research by Myhill (1999) raises questions, since the increase in the use of unseen exams in English has been accompanied by a more rapid improvement in girls' performance than that of boys.

It remains to be seen whether a recent move away from coursework will narrow the **gender gap**.

Reasons for improvement in girls' achievement: Conclusion

As well as the above factors, the relative improvement of females in education could partly be explained by the relative decline of males, which is discussed in the next section.

Gender and achievement: Boys

Boys' underachievement in perspective

The relative **underachievement** of boys in the education system has been a matter of increasing concern. However, boys' performance in education has in fact been improving, but just not as quickly as that of girls. Francis and Skelton (2005) believe that concern over this issue has been an exaggerated '**moral panic**' – a sudden and illogical outburst about a supposed decline in society that does not reflect reality.

However:

- There is evidence that certain boys are underachieving. **Working-class** boys still tend to do very poorly in the education system.
- There has been a widening of the gender gap – the difference in performance between males and females.

This suggests that there is some problem to explain.

Changes in the labour market

Although females have benefited from changes in the labour market, in comparison, males have tended to become disadvantaged.

- A decline in manufacturing industry has led to a reduction in the **availability** of manual jobs, which are predominantly done by men.
- There has been a rise in the proportion of service sector jobs, which are predominantly done by women.
- An increase in part-time and temporary jobs may be more suited to women, who combine childcare with paid work, than to men seeking full-time employment in order to act as the primary **breadwinner** in a household.
- An increase in long-term unemployment tends to affect men more than women.

All of the above may reduce the motivation of working-class boys in particular, who may see little likelihood of occupational success. The decline or disappearance of some of the roles, which in the past defined being masculine – such as being a breadwinner or doing a manual job – is sometimes described as part of a **crisis in masculinity**.

Boys in the education system

A variety of research suggests that the relative lack of success of boys stems from the interaction between the culture of masculinity and the education system.

Research by Francis (2000) suggests that both genders face problems in education, but there are a number of problems specific to boys. These are:

1. Boys get more classroom attention from teachers but are criticized more by teachers than girls. This can demotivate them and lower their expectations.
2. In the 1970s, boys tended to think that they were more able than girls. Changing teacher attitudes and publicity about male underachievement have led to boys losing their confidence.
3. The stereotype of the ideal pupil tends to fit girls better than boys.

Girls may seem more organized and be more conscientious than boys. If boys are labelled as a problem, this can lead to a **self-fulfilling prophecy** where their behaviour becomes worse and their achievement declines.

4. Boys are generally keen to remain popular with their **peer group** and do not wish to risk being known as 'swots', 'nerds' or 'geeks' by being seen to work too hard at school.

Key study
Jackson: Laddish culture

Jackson (2006) used interviews and questionnaires to study masculinity and femininity in eight schools. She found:

- The schools were dominated by a culture of **hegemonic** (or dominant) masculinity which valued toughness, power and competitiveness.
- Academic work was seen as being essentially feminine and therefore 'uncool' by boys.
- Boys tended to mess around to impress their peer group rather than concentrating on the work – acting out a culture of laddish masculinity.
- Some boys did want to succeed but, to avoid being seen as 'uncool', worked mainly at home. This disadvantaged working-class boys who had poorer facilities at home; for example, less space to study or limited access to a computer or the internet.
- Working-class boys were particularly affected by changes in the labour market. Lacking the prospect of employment to give them a sense of identity, laddish behaviour was used to restore a sense of masculine pride.

Examiners' notes

The interaction of laddish culture with what happens inside the education system seems to be very important and needs discussing in any longer answers on this topic.

Other factors operating inside the education system are identified by Mitsos and Browne (1998). They argue that:

- Teachers now have low expectations of boys. They expect them to be disruptive and their work to be late and rushed. They therefore tend not to push boys to do better when they are underperforming.
- Boys may become disillusioned with education in their early years. Primary school environments tend to be female-dominated and may have an excessive emphasis on being neat and tidy, which are not boys' strengths.

Conclusion

Feminists such as Osler (2006) believe that the current concern about underachievement by boys has led to a neglect of the problem of underachievement among girls. For example, when pupils are excluded from school more help is now available for boys than for girls.

The emphasis on underachievement by boys could also obscure the importance of social class, since it is largely working-class boys who underachieve.

Examiners' notes

You could structure a 20-mark answer around the contrasting views of feminists and those who do see male underachievement as a serious problem. As well as theory, you can then include analysis and balanced evaluation.

The hidden curriculum

The **formal curriculum** involves the subjects, which are on the school timetable, such as English, history and physics. The hidden curriculum exists alongside this formal curriculum and involves the hidden, informal messages and lessons that come from the way schooling is organized and run. These messages are reflected in the overall ethos of the school, which in turn influences the kinds of behaviours and attitudes that are valued and rewarded and also those, which are looked down on and can lead to punishment.

Example	Hidden message/value
The school is based on a hierarchy with the headteacher having most power and pupils having very little power	People should not expect to have much control over their own lives but should accept direction from above
Men hold most senior positions in a school, while most cleaners are women	It is normal for men to be dominant in society
Pupils are rewarded for punctuality and punished for being late	Conformity to strict rules is valued above other attributes

Table 7
Examples of the hidden curriculum

Some perspectives are critical of the hidden curriculum, while others see it as an invaluable and integral part of schooling.

Functionalism and the hidden curriculum

As discussed on page 4, **functionalists** believe that education teaches attitudes and values, which are beneficial to society as a whole. These values help society to function smoothly and education helps to integrate members into society.

According to Durkheim (1961), school teaches:

- a sense of belonging and commitment to a bigger society
- a shared belief in the importance of cooperation
- school assemblies, team games and anything that produces a sense of pride in a pupil's individual school helps to pass on these values.

According to Parsons (1961) school teaches:

- a belief that individual achievement should be based on merit
- a belief in individual competition through which individuals learn to make the maximum possible contribution to society.

The exam system plays a particularly important role in this.

Marxism and the hidden curriculum

Marxists criticize functionalists by arguing that the hidden curriculum benefits the **ruling class** and not society as a whole.

Key study
Bowles and Gintis: Capitalism and the hidden curriculum

As discussed on page 7, the Marxists Bowles and Gintis (1976) believe that the main role of the hidden curriculum is to produce a docile, easily manipulated and exploitable workforce for capitalists. This is achieved in the following ways:

- High grades are awarded to pupils who conform rather than those who think critically and creatively.
- Schools are based on a hierarchy in which pupils obey teachers. This gets them accustomed to the obedience that will be necessary towards managers.
- School teaches that you should not expect to feel fulfilled in your daily activities. School is boring and this is preparation for work in capitalism, which is also boring and alienating.
- You are taught instead to be motivated by external rewards such as exam success or a pay packet.
- Rather than teaching a sense of commitment to a social group, school divides pupils, as they compete with one another. This prevents the collectivist outlook that is important for the development of trade unions.

Feminism and the hidden curriculum
Feminists agree with Marxists that the hidden curriculum does not serve the interests of society as a whole, but instead benefits a particular group. However, unlike Marxists, they see the hidden curriculum as promoting **patriarchal** values that ensure the dominance of men in society.

Michelle Stanworth (1983) found that education gave the following messages to women.

- Males are more important than females.
- Boys' careers are more important than girls' careers. (Teachers encouraged boys more than girls in pursuing careers.)
- Boys are cleverer than girls.
- Senior positions in education are disproportionately held by men. This reinforces the message that males are and should be dominant.

The hidden curriculum: Evaluation
There is no doubt that schools have a hidden curriculum, but how consistent this is and how far it is accepted by pupils is more open to debate.

- **Neo-Marxists** such as Giroux (1984) see schools as **sites of ideological struggle**. A variety of groups compete to influence education and they do not always share the same values.
- Paul Willis (1977) points out that many pupils do not accept the values promoted by the school and some rebel completely against those values by forming **anti-school subcultures**.
- Individual perspectives tend to generalize about the hidden curriculum of schools. For example, some schools and individual teachers may actively promote equality between the sexes and therefore not support a patriarchal hidden curriculum.

Examiners' notes
In 20-mark questions, comparing and contrasting the views of different perspectives on the hidden curriculum is an excellent way to demonstrate the analytical and evaluative skills necessary to get into the top mark band.

Essential notes
Additional evaluation of this study can be found on p 7.

Essential notes
Subject choice may reflect a hidden curriculum that portrays some subjects as being more masculine and others as being more feminine. The sex of teachers of different subjects, whether males or females are depicted in textbooks or even if (supposedly more feminine) group work is included in classroom teaching, are all influences.

Examiners' notes
These points are valuable for including evaluation and balance in any 12- or 20-mark answers on this topic.

Pupil subcultures

Subcultures

A **subculture** is a group within a wider **culture**, which to some extent has distinctive attitudes, **values**, **norms** or lifestyles from the wider culture within which it is embedded.

If a school as a whole can be seen as having one dominant culture with its own distinct ethos, then subcultures are groups to which a minority belong and which differ significantly from the dominant culture. All subcultures encourage loyalty and the sense of identity from members of the subculture. In return, members are given **status** by their **peers** within the group.

Hargreaves (1967) believed that the main reason that subcultures form is so that pupils who receive little status within the school as a whole can gain status by forming or belonging to a subculture in which they are valued. He found that lower-**stream** boys tended to form their own subcultures in which they could get status for defying school rules and opposing its culture.

The basis of subculture formation

Subcultures can be partly or wholly based on a number of social divisions that exist either in the wider society or within schools. These can include:

- **Class** background – working-class and middle-class pupils may form different subcultures
- **Gender** – both male and female subcultures
- **Ethnicit**y – Asian, African-Caribbean or white subcultures
- **Sets** or **streams** – higher and lower sets or streams often have distinctive subcultures
- **Youth culture** – for example, a distinctive 'goth' subculture within a school
- Sexuality – gay and straight subcultures

Often a combination of these factors all work together; for example, when a subculture is dominated by white, working-class, male pupils.

Male subcultures

Many studies have concentrated on anti-school subcultures, which have been formed by academic failures who have become hostile to a school because they gain little status from teachers.

For example, Willis (1977) distinguished the anti-school 'lads' and the pro-school 'ear 'oles'. The 'lads' were white, working-class, male and in the lower streams, whereas the 'ear 'oles' were generally middle class. Willis therefore identified a clear dichotomy between two opposite subcultures. Other sociologists, however, have identified more complex subcultural divisions.

> **Key study**
>
> **Mac an Ghaill: The variety of male subcultures**
>
> Máirtín Mac an Ghaill (1994), in a study of boys in secondary education, identified five distinct subcultures.
>
> 1. 'Academic achievers' – bought into the idea of being upwardly mobile through working hard.

Examiners' notes

Look out for 6- or 12-mark questions about types of subcultures or reasons why subcultures form.

Examiners' notes

Emphasize that Willis believed that class divisions in the wider society led to the formation of subcultures, and that processes within school reflected these wider structures.

2. 'Macho lads' – opposed to the values of the school and the authority of teachers and saw the academic achievers as effeminate.
3. 'New enterprisers' – were pro-school but were keener on vocational education as a path to success.
4. 'Real Englishman' – a small group of mainly middle-class pupils from highly educated backgrounds who valued education for its own sake.
5. Gay students – critical of the homophobia of school.

Female subcultures

Most studies have concentrated on male subcultures within schools, but there have also been some studies of female subcultures. Griffin (1985) found that girls were less likely than boys to form larger subcultures. Her research suggested that girls were more likely to form small friendship groups.

Scott Davies: Exaggerated femininity

Scott Davies (1995), in a Canadian study, did find evidence of anti-school female subcultures. The members had an exaggerated sexuality – emphasizing boyfriends and prioritizing marriage and childbearing over academic success.

Ethnicity and subcultures

Some studies have found a tendency for male African-Caribbean pupils to form anti-school subcultures because they may suffer racism, tend to be placed in lower streams and are more likely to be excluded from school than their white counterparts. However, research by Sewell (1997) suggests a more complex picture.

Key study
Tony Sewell: African-Caribbean subcultures

In a study of an all-boys school, Sewell found the following subcultures:

1. Conformists – accepted the values of the school and tried to succeed through education.
2. Innovators – wanted to succeed but disliked the process of schooling. They did not seek approval from teachers but they did try to keep themselves out of trouble.
3. Retreatists – individuals who tended to keep themselves to themselves and didn't join the other subcultures.
4. Rebels – strongly rejected the school, and were aggressively masculine.

Conclusion

- A variety of factors can form the basis for subcultures and there can be a variety of subcultures within any school.
- Not all individual pupils belong to a subculture.
- Academic success and attitudes towards it form an important element in defining different types of subculture, whether based on class, ethnicity or gender.

Examiners' notes

Use this study to illustrate the point that subcultures are not necessarily either entirely pro or anti the dominant culture of schools. Include extra analysis and evaluation to help you get into the top band.

Examiners' notes

Include some discussion of female subcultures for a balanced answer.

Essential notes

Pages 21–22 include a detailed explanation of the factors outside education which Sewell believes leads to the formation of these subcultures. However, his research has its critics who argue that racism within schools is much more important.

Teacher–pupil relationships and school organization

Teacher expectations

There is a good deal of research, which suggests that teachers tend to classify or **label** pupils, often on the basis of limited information.

As discussed on pages 18–19 interactionist theory suggests that a label, which defines someone as a particular type of person can affect a person's perception of themselves, or their **self-concept**. This in turn can shape a person's behaviour and result in a self-fulfilling prophecy. When a teacher predicts that a pupil will do well or poorly, they communicate this belief to the pupil in some way; this affects the self-concept of the pupil and the pupil lives up to the expectations of the teacher.

Key study

Rosenthal and Jacobson: The self-fulfilling prophecy

In a famous study, Rosenthal and Jacobson (1968) tested the theory of the self-fulfilling prophecy using a **field experiment**. In a state primary school in California, they gave teachers false information about the IQ scores of some of the pupils. Pupils were selected at random but teachers were informed that one group was particularly bright and were expected to do very well, while another group had low IQ scores and were expected to make little progress. The study found that, in general, the pupils performed in line with the information that had been given to the teachers. Regardless of their actual IQ scores, the pupils that the teachers had been told were intelligent made much more progress than those whom they believed had low intelligence.

A large number of attempts have been made to **replicate** this research and to test the results. However, while some of these studies have found evidence to support Rosenthal and Jacobson, many have not found evidence that labelling produces a significant effect.

The ideal pupil and ability

Relationships between teachers and pupils can be shaped by teachers' conceptions of the ideal pupil.

- Research suggests that teachers see the ideal pupil as one who conforms to **middle-class** standards of behaviour – those who are cooperative and hard-working, polite and unlikely to challenge the teacher.
- The ideal pupil is also seen as one who clearly has ability, that is, the potential to do well.
- Research by Gillborn and Youdell (2001) has found that when judging pupils, teachers tend to see ability as fixed. They therefore tend to believe that some pupils have limited potential.
- Gillborn and Youdell found in their research that middle-class and white pupils were much more likely than other pupils to fit the image of the ideal pupil, and therefore to be seen as having high ability.

- Pupils who did not fit the ideal were more likely to have their behaviour judged negatively, and to be placed in lower sets or to be excluded from school.
- This led to poor relationships between teachers and some ethnic minority pupils. In particular, it led to hostility from some African-Caribbean boys.

The organization of teaching and learning

As discussed on page 18, the allocation of pupils to different groups can have an effect on educational progress. The main ways of organizing pupils into different groups are as follows:

1. **mixed ability** – groups where pupils of all abilities are taught together in a single class
2. **streaming** – pupils taught in separate groups for all subjects, based on what is believed to be their overall ability level
3. **setting** – pupils are placed in particular groups according to their perceived ability in specific subjects
4. **within-class groupings** – pupils placed in different groups; for example, on different tables within a class, and given different work to do.

All ways of allocating pupils to different groups can affect the self-concept of individuals and their level of confidence.

Research by Gillborn, Mirza and Youdell (2000) found that black pupils were often placed in lower sets, even when they had demonstrated as much ability as some white pupils placed in higher sets (see page 22).

Key study

Hallam et al.: Teaching and learning in primary schools

Hallam et al. (2004) studied six primary schools with different ways of organizing teaching and learning. This included those that used mixed ability and others that used streaming.

They found that:

- Most pupils preferred whole-class or individual work rather than having within-class groupings, as they disliked feeling left out.
- Children in mixed ability groups were better adjusted and had better attitudes to peers than those in streamed schools.
- Negative attitudes to those in the lower streams were common, and pupils in lower streams often had fewer friends than those in high streams.

In a review of research into secondary schooling, Hallam et al. found evidence that streaming played a major role in creating pro- and **anti-school subcultures**. Also, on balance, they found that setting seems to have a negative impact on performance in maths.

Conclusion

Research suggests that different ways of organizing schooling does not have much impact on overall results, but it does tend to create greater inequality between the performance of more able and less able pupils.

Educational policy before 1979

The start of state education

Before 1870, some elementary education was provided by churches and charities, and children could attend fee-paying **public schools** or selective grammar schools for secondary education. A third of children received no education at all.

In 1870 the Education Act provided state schools for all five to 11-year-olds and, in 1880, state education was made compulsory up to the age of 10.

In 1902 Local Education Authorities (**LEAs**) were established and the number of grammar schools was expanded. Although grammar schools still charged fees, some **working-class** children who passed a scholarship exam were given free education.

The 1944 Education Act

In 1944 state education was completely reorganized, with the intention of providing a comprehensive and free education for everybody up to the age of 15.

The 1944 Act established three types of secondary school under the **tripartite system**, as shown in **table 8**. This was based on the assumption that different types of pupil were better suited to different types of education. The differences were based on what was seen to be an innate ability, which was believed to be fixed and measurable at the age of 11, using intelligence tests or **IQ tests**.

The IQ test given to pupils was known as the 11+. It consisted of questions that were supposed to measure the abstract reasoning ability of pupils.

Essential notes

Functionalists link the expansion of education to the requirement of industrial societies for more skilled workers in a more complex division of labour.

Essential notes

Some of the research supporting the view that intelligence is innate and can be measured in IQ tests was conducted by Sir Cyril Burt. His work was later discredited when it was discovered that he had falsified some of the data.

Examiners' notes

Only include a discussion of these policies if the question asks you to go this far back in time. If it asks about policies in the last 30 years, the tripartite system is not relevant.

Type of institution	Basis of admission	Type of education	Typical pupils
Grammar school	Passing an IQ test (the 11+). Provided for around 20% of pupils	Academic education – often included classics	Mainly middle-class. In some areas, more places for boys than girls
Secondary modern school	Failing 11+ and lacking aptitude in technical subjects. Provided for around 75% of pupils	Less academic than grammar schools, much more emphasis on practical and vocational subjects	Mainly working-class
Technical school	Aptitude for technical subjects. Provided for around 5% of pupils	Emphasizing technical, vocational skills	Variety of backgrounds, particularly skilled working-class; more boys than girls

Table 8
The tripartite system

Criticisms of the tripartite system

1. Many critics argued that the 11+ did not truly measure ability. It was also argued that 11 was too young to measure ability.
2. The different types of school were not regarded as having equal status.
3. Fewer places were provided in grammar schools for girls than boys, even though girls tended to score higher in the 11+ exam.
4. From a **social democratic** perspective (see page 10), the system was socially divisive, since grammar schools were predominantly middle class and secondary moderns predominantly working class.

The introduction of comprehensives

Partly because of the criticisms put forward by social democrats, comprehensive schools started to be introduced in the 1960s. Comprehensives developed as a result of the policies of the Labour governments who were in power from 1965 to 1970 and from 1974 to 1979. By 1979, more than 80% of children attended comprehensive schools.

Comprehensive schools were intended to:

1. break down class divisions by ensuring that people from all classes were educated in the same sort of school
2. create more **equal opportunities**, since no one would be disadvantaged by being sent to second-class schools.

Evaluation of comprehensives

The introduction of comprehensives was controversial and some critics, particularly Conservative Party supporters, argued that they were ineffective. Their objections were:

1. Comprehensives lowered standards by undermining the excellent academic education offered in grammar schools. The most able did not have their ability stretched and the poor behaviour of the less able dragged down those who wanted to work hard and succeed.
2. Comprehensives had poor discipline, which made progress for all children problematic.
3. They were less successful than grammar schools in offering academic education to talented working-class children. It was believed that some members of the working class got more chance to be **upwardly socially mobile** through attendance at schools with an academic emphasis.

Some supporters of social democratic policies also felt that comprehensives were a failure: the introduction of **streaming** and **setting** reproduced academic and class divisions within the schools. The higher academic sets were generally middle class, while the non-academic, lower sets were mainly working class.

However, there is some evidence that comprehensives did not lead to a lowering of standards. For example, the proportion of the population gaining A-levels and higher grade O-levels (now GCSEs) increased.

Examiners' notes

If you are answering essay questions on the development of policy, link these criticisms to the social democratic perspective and continuing political debates about the best way to organize education.

Examiners' notes

Develop these points by referring to all the evidence of continuing differences in achievement by social class (see page 18).

Educational policy, 1979 to 1997

The Conservatives and the New Right

As discussed on page 10, the **New Right** (also sometimes called **neo-liberals** or market liberals) believe that state-run services tend to be inefficient. They argue that a **free market**, in which companies compete for business, provides incentives for improvement in the quality of services over time. Expenditure by the state that they see as unnecessary or excessive is a drain on the economy, since it must be paid for out of taxes that ultimately come from the profits of companies.

They believe that the introduction of market forces, competition and choice into education can lead to greater **efficiency** and improve standards by creating a more skilled workforce. They are therefore in favour of the **marketization** of education – creating a market in education, just as there is a market for the products of private businesses.

The New Right was not in favour of making all pupils attend comprehensive schools since this limited choice, restricted competition and, in their view, lowered standards and undermined academic education. They were in favour of a greater emphasis on **vocational** education for pupils who were not academic so that they would leave education with the skills required by employers. To the New Right, the purpose of education was to promote economic growth by raising standards and training the workforce, rather than to try to produce greater equality or eradicate class differences.

The New Right and educational reform

The Conservative governments of Margaret Thatcher and John Major (1979 to 1997) were strongly influenced by New Right philosophy.

Significant reforms in schooling were introduced in the 1988 Education Reform Act. **Table 9** summarizes the main provisions of this Act.

Policy	Details of policy	Purpose of policy	Problems/criticisms
Formula funding and open enrolment	School admissions were not controlled by Local Education Authorities (LEAs) and schools could enrol as many pupils as they could physically fit into the buildings. Parents given more choice of school. Funding based on the number of pupils attracted	Competition would drive up standards. Popular schools could expand, so more pupils got a good education. Poorer schools had to improve or teachers' jobs were at risk	Schools in **middle-class** areas tended to be better than those in **working-class** areas. Popular schools tended to be **oversubscribed**, so many people did not get their first choice. Middle classes manipulated the system to their advantage

Policy	Details of policy	Purpose of policy	Problems/criticisms
National Curriculum	The government stipulates most of the curriculum content, with detailed targets for achievement of pupils at different key stages	To ensure that basic skills (e.g. English, maths and science) are taught consistently, so school leavers are employable. To provide a common basis for measuring progress and evaluating school performance	The National Curriculum restricted choice of subjects designed to meet local needs/interests. Some saw a cultural bias in the content, (e.g. a lack of concern with issues of interest to minority ethnic groups)
Testing and attainment targets	Performance tests introduced at ages seven, 11, 14 and 16	To provide information at all levels of school education and to focus the efforts of schools on achieving key targets	Amount of testing seen to be excessive and led to schools focusing too much on tests
Introduction of league tables and regular, published inspections	League tables were introduced to judge the performance of schools. School inspections became more frequent and the reports more easily accessible to parents	To provide information to parents so that they could make rational decisions about choice of school. To make schools more accountable and therefore drive up standards	Schools that can attract more able pupils have a built-in advantage. League tables measure a limited range of outcomes and schools focus on achieving league table success rather than broader educational objectives
Introduction of new types of school	Existing schools could become grant-maintained – funded directly by government rather than the local education authority. **City Technology Colleges**, situated in inner cities, were partly funded by the private sector. They emphasized maths, science and technology	Intended to provide more choice and greater variety in the education system, to encourage further competition	Grant-maintained schools were a way of reintroducing selection, which mainly benefited the middle class. Seen as designed to reduce the power of Labour-run councils as much as to improve education

Table 9
The Education Reform Act, 1988

☞ This topic continues on the next two pages

Examiners' notes

This is a useful study for evaluating the policies of all recent governments promoting competition within education. Reference to specific research can help you get into the top mark band on 12- and 20-mark questions by adding depth to the analysis and evaluation.

Key study

Stephen Ball et al.: Educational choice and markets

Stephen Ball et al. (1994) conducted studies of the effects of the educational reforms introduced by Margaret Thatcher's Conservative government. They found that some groups took more advantage of the introduction of markets than others.

- Middle-class parents were usually **privileged/skilled choosers**. They had the time and social contacts to make informed choices about which were the best schools. Many had the money to move home to be in the catchment area for the most successful state schools or to pay for private education if necessary.
- Working-class parents were usually **disconnected choosers**. With limited access to private transport, they often chose the local school and based decisions on the happiness of their children rather than the academic reputation of the school.

The new policies had a number of negative effects on the education system.

- All schools tried hard to attract the most academically able students to boost league table results.
- Less attention was paid to students with special educational needs.
- Time and resources were devoted to improving school image to attract pupils.
- Cooperation between neighbouring schools became less common.
- Most schools tried to portray a traditional academic image; for example, by enforcing rules about school uniform, so there was little real choice for parents.

Evaluation of marketization in schooling

Critics of the reforms argue that they reintroduced and strengthened class divisions within the education system.

Bartlett and Le Grand (1993) see the system as resulting in **cream-skimming** – the most successful schools in the wealthiest areas are able to attract the most able students from the most affluent backgrounds. As schools increasingly set their own selection criteria, they could find ways to choose 'respectable' and hard-working pupils for their schools; for example, by insisting that applicants have regularly attended a religious institution. Schools started to choose parents rather than parents choosing schools.

New vocationalism

New vocationalism involved a renewed emphasis on training individuals for particular jobs or vocations. The New Right believed that many school leavers were unemployable and this was restricting Britain's economic growth. Education had become too dominated by the beliefs of left-wing educational professionals, and employers had too little input into the content of education. A number of measures were introduced.

Essential notes

Cream-skimming has also become possible with the introduction of specialist schools (under New Labour), and **academies** and **Free Schools** under the coalition government.

- YTS (the Youth Training Scheme) – a two-year course that combined work experience with education. It was aimed at unemployed young people who were thought to lack basic skills. Employers were paid to take, and train, unemployed youths.
- NVQs (National Vocational Qualifications) – qualifications that laid down standards in particular occupations. These were often studied part-time in colleges while students worked in the occupation.
- GNVQs (General National Vocational Qualifications) – broader alternatives to academic courses that prepared pupils for work in a general occupational area such as leisure and tourism.
- Modern Apprenticeships – combined work-based training with attendance at college to help young workers achieve NVQ qualifications.

Criticisms of new vocationalism

Phil Cohen (1984) saw the real purpose of vocational training as the creation of attitudes that made young people easily exploited workers. If they did not join training schemes and conform to the requirements of the schemes, they were disciplined by the threat of having benefits removed. The skills taught were only suitable for very low-paid and low-skilled jobs.

Dan Finn (1987) criticized training schemes for offering cheap labour for employers, who provided little real training. He believed the real purpose was to manipulate unemployment statistics by taking people off the register and also to undermine trade union power, since trainees were unlikely to be members of unions. Finn denied that school leavers were unemployable, since most had already worked part-time. The real problem was simply a lack of jobs in the economy.

Conclusion

Although various aspects of the reforms introduced by the New Right were heavily criticized, many of them were retained when a New Labour government was elected in 1997. Some aspects of the policies were then developed even further. The Conservative members of the coalition government formed in 2010 (see page 43) were also sympathetic to many of the aims of the New Right, so the New Right approach has had a lasting influence on British education.

Examiners' notes

Look out for 6- and 12-mark questions specifically about vocational education. You may also need to include details of policies under subsequent governments.

Educational policy since 1997

New Labour

From 1997 to 2010 the Labour Party was in power, first under the leadership of Tony Blair and then, from 2007, under Gordon Brown.

Before taking power, the leadership of the Labour Party had begun describing themselves as **New Labour** to signal that they were no longer following traditional Labour Party policies. The New Labour philosophy was to follow a **Third Way**. This was neither the traditional left wing of the old Labour Party, nor the **right-wing** approach of the **New Right**, but mixed policies from both sides of the political spectrum.

Policies influenced by social democratic philosophy

Some education policies drew on the left-wing philosophy of the social democratic approach. These aimed to produce greater equality of opportunity by providing additional help or opportunity to those from poorer backgrounds.

Essential notes

The Third Way was partly devised by the sociologist Anthony Giddens, an adviser to Tony Blair. It claimed to follow a coherent philosophy, based on free markets, with some government intervention to make society fairer, but critics felt it lacked a clear direction.

Details of policy	Purpose of policy
Excellence in Cities	
Extra resources provided for education in disadvantaged inner-city areas. Included learning centres with IT facilities, learning mentors, and units for children at risk of exclusion	To improve results for disadvantaged children by helping them to overcome economic and social disadvantage
Sure Start	
Provided extra help for pre-school children in deprived areas (e.g. play centres and home visits to advise parents on pre-school education)	To create more equal opportunity through intervening early to boost the long-term educational performance of deprived children
Academies	
New schools, partly sponsored by businesses, set up to replace failing comprehensive schools	To ensure that no children, particularly those in poorer areas, were educated in a very ineffective school
Further education expansion and Education Maintenance Allowances	
FE was expanded and participation rates increased. EMAs provided payments of up to £30 a week to children from less affluent homes continuing in education after school	To provide more opportunities in post-compulsory education for those from working-class backgrounds. EMAs were intended to reduce drop-out rates by making it more affordable to stay on in education
Expansion of higher education	
Number of places in higher education was increased rapidly, nearly doubling between 1990 and 2004	To increase opportunities for people from all class backgrounds, but particularly those from the working class

Essential notes

Excellence in Cities and Sure Start are examples of compensatory education – additional education to help compensate the deprived for their disadvantages.

Table 10
New Labour education policies promoting equality

Policies influenced by New Right philosophy

Other policies introduced by New Labour drew on the philosophy of the New Right. These were more concerned with raising standards, making education more competitive and increasing apparent choice.

Details of policy	Purpose of policy
Specialist schools	
Schools could specialize in one of 10 areas (e.g. computing, science, sports, humanities) and select up to 10% of pupils according to aptitude in the specialism	To increase choice as opposed to everyone going to standard comprehensive schools. Increased institutional diversity to meet the needs of individual pupils

Essential notes

Value-added league tables were designed to take into account differences in student intake, but the tables with the raw exam performance figures are used more by the media and parents.

Details of policy	Purpose of policy
Use of league tables	
League tables continued to be used and more details published, including 'value-added' scores based on progress	To drive up standards by fostering competition and to measure progress towards government targets. Value-added league tables intended to provide a fairer measure of schools' performance by taking some account of class differences
New Deal for Young People	
Provided education, training, voluntary work or subsidized jobs for unemployed young people as well as support from personal advisers	To prevent young people joining the ranks of the long-term unemployed
Vocational GCSEs and A-levels	
NVQs were changed into vocational GCSEs and A-levels in 2001	To improve the status of vocational qualifications, so they were not seen as second-rate compared with academic qualifications

Examiners' notes

In some questions you might need to discuss the merits of league tables. Critics argue that they simply advantage the schools that are able to attract the most able and highest proportion of higher-class pupils.

Table 11
New Labour education policies encouraging competition and choice

Evaluation of New Labour policies

Tomlinson (2005) criticizes these policies for:

- reintroducing selection through specialist schools; this favoured the middle class who were better able to get their children into **oversubscribed schools**
- an over-emphasis on targets and league tables, leading to a narrow focus within education.

Although higher education was expanded, the introduction of student fees may have discouraged some people from studying for a degree.

Trowler (2003) believes New Labour underestimated the degree to which inequality in society prevents equality of opportunity in education.

McKnight et al. (2005), however, found that overall standards have risen, with improvements in GCSE, A-level and key stage tests, and a small reduction in class differences in achievement at school.

The coalition government from 2010

After the general election of 2010, a coalition government was formed. This was made up mainly of Conservatives but with the support of the Liberal Democrats.

Most of the early policies emphasized competition and choice.

- Introduction of Free schools so that charities, businesses, teachers and parents could start their own state-funded schools to compete with existing schools.
- Schools could leave LEA control and become academies. These continued to be state-funded but had increased control over their own affairs.

Money was saved by scrapping EMAs (allowance paid to children from poorer homes staying on in further education). University tuition fees were increased to up to £9 000 per year.

Largely as a result of Liberal Democrat influence, some policies were introduced that were designed to create greater opportunity for poorer groups. The Pupil Premium provided £7 billion to help raise the achievement of children from disadvantaged backgrounds.

Essential notes

Keep up-to-date on the latest policies by following the news, add key details to your notes and think about how the policies fit different perspectives on education. A useful source is the BBC website education section – www.bbc.co.uk/news/education.

Examiners' notes

Examiners will always be impressed by knowledge of relevant contemporary events in answers to 12- and 20-mark questions.

Varieties of data and research methods

The purpose of research
Social research can be conducted for a number of purposes.

- It can be used to test existing theories. Researchers conduct **experiments** to test a particular **hypothesis** (a prediction about what is likely to happen). They decide whether the hypothesis is supported or contradicted, based on their **observations** of the results of these experiments.
- It can be used to develop new theories. By observing social life, the researcher can produce new ideas about how some aspects of society works or what causes particular types of social behaviour.

Methodology is concerned with the methods used to collect data and the philosophy underlying the production of sociological data.

Types of data
Research can involve producing or using different types of data.

1. **Quantitative data** consists of data in a numerical form; for example, statistics about the number of males and females passing an exam.
2. **Qualitative data** is any data that is not numerical; for example, written descriptions, diaries, photographs, recorded music or radio programmes.

Data sources can be divided into two types.

1. **Primary sources** are those sources of data that are produced directly by the sociologist conducting research; for example, resulting from a **questionnaire** or **interview**.
2. **Secondary sources** consist of existing data produced by someone else but used by the sociologist.

Examiners' notes
This section introduces basic terms, which you may be asked to explain for a 2-mark question. You need to be able to define the terms highlighted in bold.

Type of data	Primary source	Secondary source
Quantitative	Numerical data from research conducted by a sociologist (e.g. statistics from a questionnaire)	Existing numerical data (e.g. official government statistics)
Qualitative	Non-numerical data from a sociological study (e.g. notes on the observation of a classroom)	Non-numerical data from existing material (e.g. content of diaries or email messages)

Table 12
Types of data

Many individual studies use a mixture of qualitative and qualitative data and primary and secondary sources.

Evaluating data
No data produced by research is perfect, as all types of data have limitations. These can be considered in terms of the following concepts.

1. **Reliability**. Data is reliable if another researcher using identical methods would produce the same results. Reliable data can be checked through the research being reproduced or **replicated**;

for example, reviewing registration details of the number of people attending an event or sitting an exam. Unreliable data is data that would not be confirmed by a repeat of the same study.

2. **Validity** concerns how true data is, that is, how close the fit is between the data and reality. Data is invalid if it does not match reality. For example, invalid data might be produced if respondents to interviews do not tell the truth.

3. **Representativeness** and **generalizability**. Data is representative if the individuals or examples studied are a typical cross-section of the wider population or group that the researcher is interested in. If the individuals or examples are representative, then it is legitimate to make generalizations about the wider group they represent.

Choosing research topics

A sociologist's choice of topic to investigate is influenced by the following factors.

1. **Practical issues**

   Researchers need to choose topics for which it is feasible to develop and conduct valid research. For example, if a specific group needs to be studied in relation to a particular topic, it must be possible to identify and then get access to members of this group. Another practical consideration relates to the availability of research grants. Most researchers rely upon funding, which may come directly from research councils that distribute money from the government, charities or businesses. The choice of research topic tends to reflect the availability of funds.

2. **Ethical issues**

   Ethics concern whether research is seen as morally acceptable. Research may be seen as unethical if:
   - it harms the subjects of the research
   - the subjects are unable or unwilling to give **informed consent** (they must be aware of the research, understand it and be in a position to agree to take part)
   - it is impossible to maintain **confidentiality** by keeping the identity of the subjects secret
   - the research could be used to help individuals or organizations carry out illegal or immoral acts.

3. **Theoretical issues**

   Researchers are inevitably influenced by their own **values** about what they believe to be important. For example, **feminist** researchers are more likely to choose topics concerned with gender inequality than other types of researchers.

   The importance of a topic might relate to how it is linked to the introduction of new social policies, to understanding developments in society, or because it can be used to examine influential theories within sociology.

Essential notes

Sociological data may be reliable but invalid. For example, if data from questionnaires is accurately compiled and would be confirmed in a repeat of the questionnaire, but the respondents have not responded truthfully.

Examiners' notes

Evaluating research methods is usually the main focus of the 20-mark 'Methods in context' question, so understanding these concepts and being able to apply them is essential.

Essential notes

Theoretical issues such as the preferred perspective or approach of the sociologist might seem the most important, but in reality, practicality trumps theoretical and ethical issues; if it is impractical to carry out some research then it is unlikely to be attempted.

☞ This topic continues on the next two pages

Research methods and sources

Sociologists use a number of different research methods or sources.

- **Experiment**: Researchers set up an artificial situation and manipulate it to test their theory. Rosenthal and Jacobson (1968) tested the theory of the **self-fulfilling prophecy** by giving teachers false information about the IQ scores of pupils (see page 34).
- **Questionnaire**: A written list of questions, which are answered by respondents. J.W.B. Douglas (1970) used questionnaires alongside other methods to study the factors influencing attainment in different social classes.
- **Interview**: Verbal questioning of one or more people by a researcher. William Labov (1973) used interviews to study the linguistic ability of children.
- **Observation/participant observation**: Researcher watches an event or behaviour and records the observations. In participant observation, the researcher takes part in the events being observed. Cecile Wright (1992) conducted classroom observation to study **racism** in education.
- **Official statistics**: Numerical data produced by government agencies. McKnight et al. (2005) used data from official statistics on qualifications to evaluate the effectiveness of the Labour government's policies.
- **Documents**: Any physical artefacts containing information that could be used by a sociologist. Leon Feinstein (2003) used data from the National Child Development Study to examine factors shaping educational achievement.

Selecting research methods

Various factors influence the choice of research method; these are generally similar to the issues which affect the choice of topic.

1. **Practical** issues – for example, ease of access to the group, availability of funding and time constraints.
2. **Ethical** issues – for example, participant safety, informed consent and confidentiality.
3. **Theoretical** issues – whether the data produced will be valid and reliable.

Philosophies of research

Two broad theoretical approaches to research methods can be identified.

Positivism

Positivism is an early influential approach, advocated by Auguste Comte (1840s) and Émile Durkheim (1897), which suggests that sociology can be scientific. Positivists believe that:

- There are **objective social facts** about the social world. These facts can be expressed in statistics.
- You can look for **correlations** – patterns in which two or more things tend to occur together.

- Correlations may represent **causal relationships** (one thing causing another).
- It is possible to discover **laws** of human behaviour – causes of behaviour that are true for all humans throughout history.
- Human behaviour is shaped by external stimuli (things that happen to us) rather than internal stimuli (what goes on in the mind).
- To be scientific you should only study what you can observe; that is, not emotions, meanings or motives, which cannot be observed.
- This perspective supports the use of quantitative methods such as official statistics, which provide factual data.

The interpretive approach

Interpretivists usually advocate the use of qualitative data to interpret social action, with an emphasis on the meanings and motives of participants. From this viewpoint:

- people do not simply react to external stimuli, but interpret the **meaning** of stimuli before reacting
- an understanding of people's unobservable subjective states is required. This cannot be reduced to statistical data.

Methods therefore have to be used, which reveal these meanings, **motives**, emotions and beliefs. These include in-depth interviews and participant observation.

Not all sociologists support an exclusively interpretive or positivist approach; many use elements from both approaches. For example, they may collect statistics but also use qualitative data to understand the reasons for the behaviour, which produces the statistics.

Examiners' notes

Contrast these approaches to develop more in-depth analysis. Explain why positivists tend to criticize qualitative and subjective methods and interpretivists tend to criticize more quantitative and 'scientific' methods.

Sampling and case studies

The purpose of sampling

Instead of studying an entire **population** (the group of interest in a particular study) the researcher usually selects a small sample that is representative of the population as a whole. The sociologist can then generalize about the larger population on the basis of the group studied.

- The **sampling unit** is the individual thing or person in that population.
- The **sampling frame** is a list of all those in the population (for example, the Electoral Roll is a sampling frame of those eligible to vote).

Types of sampling

There are a variety of ways of producing a sample. **Table 13** summarizes the advantages and disadvantages of each.

Table 13
Types of sampling

Type of sampling	How it is conducted	Advantages/ Why it is used	Disadvantages
Random	Every sampling unit has an equal chance of being chosen (e.g. drawn out of a hat)	Technically, the most representative, as it relies upon statistical odds	Large sample needed to ensure that statistically it is likely to be representative
Stratified random	Population divided into groups according to important **variables** (e.g. **class**, **gender**, **ethnicity**). Sample then chosen in same proportions as found in population	Relatively small sample can be used with confidence that it is still representative	Requires sampling frame which includes details of significant characteristics of population being studied
Quota	Establishes pre-determined number of people with each particular characteristic. Once quota is filled no more people in that category are included	Advantages of stratified random sampling but can be conducted without variables being available from sampling frame	Accessibility of potential respondents affects their chances of being included in the sample. May be less representative than random and stratified random sampling
Multi-stage	Involves taking a sample of a sample (e.g. a sample of voters in a sample of constituencies)	Allows a broad-based sample while saving time and money through not including all the potential sources	Less truly representative than some methods, as many members of the population have no chance of being selected

Type of sampling	How it is conducted	Advantages/ Why it is used	Disadvantages
Snowballing	Members of a sample put researcher in touch with other potential members	Used mainly with groups who are hard to identify or access (e.g. criminals)	Very unlikely to be truly representative, since based on people who have contact with one another
Opportunity	People chosen on basis of being easily accessible and willing to participate in research	Tends to be easiest, cheapest and quickest way of collecting a sample and may lead to a good **response-rate**	Makes no attempt to be truly representative, so cannot generalize from the findings

Non-representative sampling

Members of a sample may be picked for being untypical of a population or to study specific characteristics. This **non-representative sampling** is used:

- To **falsify** (prove wrong) a general theory by looking for exceptions to a pattern. Margaret Fuller (1984) studied a sample of African-Caribbean girls who were very successful in the education system even though overall rates of success for this ethnic group were relatively low.
- To find the **key informants** who can provide information about an area of social life because they have special insights or expertise (for example, criminals).

Case studies

Another highly unrepresentative form of sampling is to use a particular **case study**. Case studies can be used:

- to develop a comprehensive understanding of something by studying it in depth
- to develop a general theoretical approach by falsifying a theory or proving it wrong
- to develop **typologies** (for example, different school subcultures)
- to generate new **hypotheses** or theories.

A problem with case studies is that you cannot generalize from them. Bryman (1988) suggests that this can be overcome through using multiple case studies. However, it can be difficult to compare the findings of case studies carried out by different researchers.

Life histories

A **life history** is a case study of one person's life. An example is Thomas and Znaniecki's (1919) study of Jenny, an ageing woman. Plummer (1982) suggests that these are useful for helping understand the world from an individual's point of view. However, they are highly unrepresentative and cannot be used to make generalizations.

Surveys and questionnaires

Social surveys

Social surveys are large-scale studies, which collect standardized data about large groups, often using **questionnaires**.

- **Factual surveys** collect descriptive information.
- **Attitudes surveys** examine subjective opinions (for example, opinion polls).
- **Explanatory surveys** test theories or produce hypotheses.

Pilot studies

A **pilot study** is a small-scale trial study conducted before the main study in order to test the feasibility of the main study and to refine the research methods being used.

They can be used to:

- test how useful and unambiguous interview questions are
- develop ways to gain the cooperation of respondents
- develop the research skills of the researchers
- decide whether or not to proceed with research.

Conducting questionnaires

Questionnaires consist of a written list of questions. When planning this type of research the researcher has to choose how to administer the questionnaire. A key consideration will be what level of response-rate is required; that is, what proportion of questionnaires need to be completed and returned. **Table 14** summarizes the options and the main advantages and disadvantages of their different approaches.

Examiners' notes

A typical 4-mark question might be to suggest two reasons why people contuct pilot studies.

Examiners' notes

20-mark essay questions about questionnaires or surveys are likely to specify a particular type. Make sure you write about the specific issues related to administering this type as well as general advantages and disadvantages.

Method of administering questionnaire	Main advantages	Main disadvantages
Face-to-face	Relatively high response-rate Interviewer can clarify questions	Interviewer may influence responses (**interviewer bias**) Time-consuming for both subject and interviewer, therefore potentially expensive
Telephone	Relatively cheap, and easy to access a geographically dispersed **sample**	Response-rates may be low, limited to subjects who are prepared to take part in telephone research Respondents may be influenced by voice of interviewer

Method of administering questionnaire	Main advantages	Main disadvantages
Postal	Relatively cheap and easy to access a geographically dispersed sample No interviewer bias from direct contact	Response-rates tend to be very low Respondents may not be typical of the population as a whole
Internet	Very cheap and quick to send to a widely dispersed sample	Response-rate is likely to be low Limited to those with internet access and not inclined to delete 'spam'

Table 14
Ways of administering questionnaires

Researchers also have to develop the questions to collect reliable data on what are often abstract concepts or theories. This is called **operationalizing** concepts (see pp 52-53). Deciding what types of questions to include and how to word them is a real skill. **Table 15** summarizes the advantages and disadvantages of different types of questions.

Type of question	Description	Advantages	Disadvantages
Fixed-choice	Respondents are given a restricted range of options to choose from (e.g. agree/disagree, yes/no) or asked to use a ratings scale (e.g. from 1 to 10)	Easy to produce statistical data and to analyse answers Good for testing existing theories and producing **reliable** data which can be checked **Positivists** see answers as **social facts**	No opportunity for respondents to clarify concepts or qualify views Generally poor for collecting information about feelings, **meanings** or **motives** Not favoured by interpretivists
Open-ended	Respondents are asked the question and can provide their own unprompted response	Can produce more in-depth data and better for discovering complex feelings, meanings or motives Preferred by interpretivists	Answers need to be interpreted to produce quantitative data Difficult and time-consuming to produce statistical data Less favoured by positivists

Essential notes

The Likert scale in fixed-choice questions measures respondents who are asked to say whether they strongly agree or agree, or strongly disagree or disagree with a statement.

Table 15
Advantages and disadvantages of fixed-choice and open-ended questions

This topic continues on the next two pages

The advantages of questionnaires

- large amounts of data can be collected quickly
- little personal involvement by researchers
- access to subjects is easy
- no great ethical issues since research cannot be conducted secretly and filling in the questionnaire implies consent
- easy to quantify the results, find correlations and use statistical analysis to look for causes
- everyone responds to the same stimuli so positivists see differences in answers as reflecting real differences
- comparative analysis and replication (repeating the questionnaire) are easy, making the results reliable
- a large, geographically dispersed sample can be used, increasing the representativeness of the data and the ability to generalize.

For positivists, the statistical patterns revealed can be used to develop new theories; and questionnaires can be devised to test existing theories.

Non-positivists see questionnaires as useful for collecting straightforward, descriptive data.

The disadvantages of questionnaires

Interpretive sociologists question the use of questionnaires for a range of reasons.

- When designing questionnaires, researchers assume that they know what is important, so find it difficult to develop novel hypotheses.
- The operationalization of concepts distorts the social world by shaping concepts that are in line with researchers' rather than respondents' meanings.
- Different answers may not reflect real differences between respondents, as they may have interpreted the questions differently.
- The validity of the data may be undermined by deliberate lying, faulty memory or respondents not fully understanding their own motivations. People may not act in line with questionnaire answers. For example, people may deny being **racist** even though they act in racist ways.
- The coding of **open-ended** data distorts the distinct answers given by individuals.
- There could be an ethical issue of confidentiality unless the questionnaires are handled carefully.
- Researchers are distant from their subjects, making it difficult to understand the social world from their viewpoint. Interaction cannot be understood through questionnaires.
- To feminist researchers, questionnaires preclude the possibility of subjects evaluating the research.

Most sociologists accept that surveys are useful for collecting factual or descriptive data, but there is controversy over their use in explanatory studies.

Examiners' notes

Discussing the advantages and disadvantages of questionnaire research is a typical 20-mark question. It is useful to break your answer down into practical, ethical and theoretical issues. Then try to include why positivists would support this type of research and interpretivists would criticize it. Use examples to get higher marks.

Operationalizing concepts

Researchers also have to develop the questions to collect valid and reliable data on what are often abstract concepts or theories. This process is called operationalizing concepts.

Operationalizing involves putting a concept in a form that allows it to be measured. This process is crucial to ensure that the concept is accurately measured (valid) and that each time they are used, every respondent understands the concept in the same way (reliable). Usually this is achieved by identifying indicators for the concept – easily measurable categories that, when put together, give a clear picture of whether or not the concept applies.

For example, asking respondents how religious they are would produce a range of answers that could not be easily compared, because respondents would understand the term 'religious' in different ways. However, the concept of 'religious' could be operationalized by identifying several indicators of being religious. These might include whether and how often the respondent attends religious services or prays, whether they believe in God(s) and religious texts, whether religious teachings affect their lifestyle and so on. The answers to these questions would need to be in a form that could be compared, so the respondent is usually given a number of fixed alternatives from which to select. This type of question is known as a closed or **fixed-choice question** – rather than freedom to write or say whatever they like – an open or **open-ended question** (see p 51).

Interviews

Structured and unstructured interviews

Interviews can be defined, simply, as one or more researchers asking questions to one or more respondents. They can have various degrees of structure depending on the extent to which the questions are pre-determined.

Degree of structure	Advantages	Disadvantages
Structured – pre-set questions asked in same order without variation	Favoured by quantitative researchers Easier to replicate and compare results Less chance of interviewer bias	No opportunity for probing deeper Less chance of discovering new hypotheses Harder to discover what is important to the respondents
Semi-structured – some fixed questions with list of topics to be covered	Provide some opportunity for respondents to lead the interviews while ensuring main topics are covered	Lacks specific advantages of both structured and unstructured interviews
Unstructured – few or no fixed questions, more like a conversation	Favoured by qualitative researchers Allow respondents to direct the interview More opportunity for developing new hypotheses	Hard to replicate Time-consuming Difficult to compare interviews May go off-track

Table 16
Degrees of structure in interviews

Interviewing styles

Most interviewers use a **non-directive** form of interviewing. In this case the interviewer offers no opinions of their own and does not express approval or disapproval of the responses. Most sociologists regard this as being the most **objective** way to interview people.

Howard Becker (1970) advocated a more aggressive style of interviewing in which the statements of the interviewees are challenged. Which interviewing Chicago school teachers he used this style to uncover some racist feelings among the teachers, which he believed they would otherwise have kept hidden.

Feminist interviewers such as Ann Oakley (1981) advocate **collaborative interviewing**. Here the researcher befriends the interviewee. Valid data emerges from the development of a relationship between the interviewer and the interviewee. Oakley sees this as the most valid and ethical type of interviewing, since she thinks more truthful data will result.

Essential notes

Feminists are generally quite hostile to positivist approaches, which they see as imposing a masculine style of research that fails to take account of the needs, interests and viewpoints of the respondents.

Type of interview	Advantages	Disadvantages
Individual	Prevents respondents from being influenced by others Less time-consuming	No opportunity to observe interaction
Group	Can observe interaction Encourages deeper thought about issues and more developed answers Closer to normal social life	Respondents may be influenced by desire to conform to views of others Dominant members of a group can sway opinion of others

Table 17
Individual and **group interviews**

Examiners' notes

Mentioning feminism can add some theoretical depth to help you reach the top mark band for 20-mark questions.

The main advantages of interviews

Both positivists and interpretivists find interviews useful. The main advantages are practicality and flexibility. **Tables 16** and **17** outline the specific advantages associated with particular types of interviews.

- Quantitative researchers prefer interviews to participant observation – larger samples can be used, statistical data can be produced with the coding of answers, and the research can be replicated to increase reliability.
- Qualitative researchers prefer interviews to questionnaires because concepts can be clarified and there is more opportunity for respondents to express ideas in their own way, say what is important to them and explore issues in depth.
- To feminists, interviews have theoretical advantages, since they provide space for critical reflection, collaboration and interaction between interviewer and interviewee.

The main disadvantages of interviews

- As with questionnaires, the validity of interview data may be affected by respondents being untruthful.
- Answers can be affected by faulty memory or people not fully understanding their own behaviour.
- Interviewers might lead respondents towards preferred answers.
- The presence of the researcher might influence answers.
- Social factors such as ethnicity may influence the sort of answers members of different social groups are willing to give.

Conclusion

The practicality and flexibility of interviews make them attractive to researchers and they are widely used. Hammersley and Gomm (2004) believe that interview data remains useful when combined with other methods but should be handled carefully.

Essential notes

Remember to use as many technical terms as possible in answers to Research Methods questions.

Examiners' notes

You can develop essays on the advantages and disadvantages of interviews with reference to examples from education (or elsewhere) and by explaining the somewhat mixed opinions of positivists and interpretivists.

Observation and participant observation

Observation

Observation simply involves looking at something and recording data.

Positivists see observation as essential; for example, when observing the results of experiments.

Interpretive sociologists are much more likely to use participant observation than positivists. They tend to use observation in the context of studying normal social life. The study of a way of life of a social group is known as ethnography.

Observation of social groups can be subjective, since the observer has to choose what exactly to take note of. However, some observers use more systematic methods to produce quantitative data. For example, Flander's Interaction Analysis Categories (FIAC) (1970) categorizes classroom interaction into 10 categories so that researchers can quantify what takes place.

Participant observation – overt and covert research

Participant observation involves the researcher joining in with the group being studied. The level to which they participate can vary.

They can be a full participant observer, or a partial participant observer.

A full participant observer:
- may develop a deeper understanding through sharing experiences
- is likely to see a full range of behaviours
- may influence the group less than an outside observer
- may find him- or herself taking part in illegal or immoral activities
- may lose objectivity and 'go native'
- may influence the group through joining in activities.

A partial participant observer:
- can easily observe groups who are different to the observer
- can commit less time to observation
- can avoid involvement in illegal or immoral activities
- may find that subjects act less naturally
- will not share the full range of group experiences.

The researcher also has to decide whether to be open (overt) or secretive (covert).

Overt participation:
- allows the observer to ask questions
- allows the observer to retain some detachment
- removes the need to lie and risk being 'uncovered'
- risks influencing the behaviour of the subjects
- makes it difficult to become a full participant
- may encounter resistance from groups not wishing to be observed.

Covert participation:
- enables respondents to act more naturally
- makes it difficult to access some groups
- can be considered unethical, as it misleads subjects

- makes it difficult to opt out of illegal or immoral activities
- can render the observer liable to lose objectivity by becoming one of the group.

The advantages of participant observation

Many sociologists regard participant observation as having a high degree of validity.

Interpretivists, in particular, support participant observation because it allows an understanding of the subjective viewpoints of individuals and the processes of interaction in which people's **meanings**, **motives** and **self-concepts** constantly change. It therefore avoids a static picture of social life. Other advantages include the following:

- can sometimes be done with little preparation and conducted by a single researcher, making the initial costs quite small
- researchers are less likely than in other methods to impose their own concepts, structures and preconceptions on the data
- may gain answers to questions that had not been anticipated and were not included in questionnaires or interviews
- difficult for respondents to lie or mislead
- researcher understands subjects better because she or he experiences some of the same things
- provides in-depth studies that can be useful both for developing new theories and for falsifying existing ones.

The limitations and disadvantages of participant observation

To positivists, participant observation is an unsystematic, subjective and unscientific method. Even for interpretivists, there are several problems:

- can be time-consuming for the researcher and may end up being costly as the researcher has to support her- or himself
- researchers' lives may be disrupted; they may need to do illegal/immoral things or they may face dangers
- can be practical difficulties about recording the data, especially in covert research when notes cannot be taken at the time
- researcher is limited to studying a small number of people in a single place
- samples are likely to be too small for generalizations
- will be impossible to join some groups to carry out observation
- studies cannot be replicated, so the results may be unreliable, and comparisons difficult
- interpretations are rather subjective as the researcher has to be very selective about what is reported
- presence of the researcher will change group behaviour and affect the validity of the data
- **covert participant observation** can be regarded as unethical because it involves lying to those being studied.

Conclusion

Participant observation is advocated by interpretivists as being the only research method that gets close to real social life and is therefore the most valid research method. It is criticized by positivists for being highly subjective, impossible to replicate, and therefore unreliable.

Examiners' notes

When answering a 20-mark question, explain why interpretivists see this as more valid than other methods because it is closer to real social life, while positivists see it as too subjective, unreliable and unscientific to be of much use. Developing these sorts of points is likely to impress the examiner.

Longitudinal research and triangulation

Longitudinal studies

Longitudinal studies involve the study of a group of people over an extended period of time. They are sometimes also known as **panel studies**. Often data is collected periodically, with the respondents being asked to provide information perhaps every few months or every few years.

Longitudinal research can use a wide range of methods; for example, periodic **focus groups** or group interviews. However, the most common method is the use of questionnaires. Longitudinal research may also make some use of **secondary sources**. An important longitudinal study into the causes of educational underachievement by the working class was conducted by J.W.B Douglas (1970).

The advantages of longitudinal research

This type of research has several advantages:

- allows the researcher to look at processes over time
- does not require respondents to recall information retrospectively, therefore the data may be more valid than conventional research
- invaluable for studying topics that look at long-term changes over an individual's **life course**; for example, looking at **social mobility**, factors influencing long-term health or the relationship between educational achievement and occupational status.

Problems with longitudinal research

There are a number of problems with conducting longitudinal research:

- requires a very long-term commitment from researchers
- because of the extended time-period, it tends to be extremely expensive
- once the research has been started, it is not possible to collect retrospective information, so a wide range of data is usually collected in the beginning, before it becomes clear what the most relevant data is going be, thus adding to the expense
- **sample** size is likely to get smaller as people drop out or disappear. Those remaining may be untypical of the sample as a whole, making it difficult to compare results over time
- sample may become less representative over time if the population it is designed to represent changes some of its characteristics
- the fact that people are taking part in a research project might make them think more about their behaviour and therefore influence the outcomes of the research, making it less valid.

Triangulation

Triangulation involves the use of three or more sources of data or research methods in the course of a single study. A researcher might use more than one primary source, and also use secondary data. Although positivists advocate the use of exclusively quantitative sources, and interpretivists prefer qualitative sources, in practice many studies combine both types of source.

Examiners' notes

There are not many examples of this type of study, because they are so time-consuming and expensive, so it is worth learning about Douglas' research to use as an example. See p 14.

Examiners' notes

This is probably most likely to crop up as a short question (2 or 4 marks), but make sure you are familiar with all these advantages and disadvantages in case you get an essay question.

Examiners' notes

Triangulation is useful for concluding discussions about any single method. Point out that each method can be complemented with other methods that provide different types of data or help to fill in the gaps.

Types of triangulation

Hammersley (1996) distinguishes three ways of combining methods:

1. Triangulation – findings are cross-checked using a variety of methods. For example, interviews are used to check the responses made in questionnaires.
2. **Facilitation** – one method is used to assist or develop the use of another method. For example, when in-depth interviews are used to devise questionnaire questions.
3. **Complementarity** – different methods are combined to dovetail different aspects of an investigation. For example, questionnaires are used to discover overall statistical patterns and participant observation is used to reveal the reasons for those patterns.

The purposes of triangulation

Bryman (2001) identifies 10 uses of triangulation.

1. To check the reliability of data produced using different methods.
2. Qualitative research facilitating quantitative research; for example, by designing questionnaire questions.
3. Quantitative research facilitating qualitative research; for example, by helping to identify people for a sample.
4. Filling in the gaps where the main research method cannot produce all the necessary data.
5. Using some methods to study static features of social life and others to study changes.
6. Using different methods to obtain different perspectives from research subjects.
7. Using different methods to help to generalize.
8. Using qualitative research to understand the relationship between **variables** revealed in the quantitative research.
9. Studying different aspects of a phenomenon.
10. Solving an unexplained result by using a different method to that initially used.

Bryman sees multi-strategy research as very useful, as the limitations and disadvantages of each individual research method can be partially overcome.

An example of triangulation

Cecile Wright (1992) used the following four combination of methods to investigate racism in primary schools:

1. Classroom observation to see how teachers actually behaved.
2. Examination of documents about test results to examine the effects of racism.
3. Interviews with headteachers to investigate school policies.
4. Informal interviews with teachers to uncover unobservable attitudes.

Essential notes

Triangulation is becoming increasingly common in sociology as it becomes more and more accepted that neither quantitative nor qualitative data can provide a full picture. Positivist and interpretivist approaches tend to lend themselves to different research questions and different topics, so they can often complement each other rather than being mutually exclusive.

Examiners' notes

You can argue that each research method is useful for certain types of study but research is usually strengthened by the use of more than one method.

Examiners' notes

This study uses several methods, so it can be used to illustrate a range of individual methods as applied to education.

Secondary sources and official statistics

Types of secondary sources and documents

Secondary sources are data that already exist. Secondary source documents can be any physical artefact that contains meaningful material produced by people. This includes images, sounds and digital data, as well as printed documents with words and statistics.

- Documents may be produced by agencies such as the government, research bodies or companies (**public documents**), or individuals (**personal documents**).
- They can be quantitative (for example, government statistics) or qualitative (for example, letters and diaries).
- They can be historical or contemporary.

The uses of secondary sources

Secondary sources are usually used for practical reasons.

- They save time and money, since they already exist and therefore do not require expensive primary research.
- Many secondary sources include data that are beyond the scope of sociologists to collect (for example, **census** data).
- They allow the study of societies in the past for which it is impossible to produce primary sources.
- They allow insights into aspects of social life that may not be accessible to researchers (for example, intimate family life).

A major disadvantage of secondary sources is that they are produced by non-sociologists for their own purposes. Therefore they may not include the specific data that sociologists are interested in, or the data may be collected without the rigour that sociologists use.

- They may use categories or concepts that do not fit with sociological theories.
- The categories used may change, making comparisons over time difficult. For example, the government has changed definitions of poverty and unemployment.

Government statistics

Government statistics cover a wide range of topics including demography, crime, unemployment, educational achievement and participation, births, deaths, marriages and divorce. The government also conducts statistical surveys such as the General Household Survey. Since 1801 it has carried out a census every decade, in which participation is compulsory.

Positivist views of official statistics

Positivists generally view official statistics as both valid and reliable. Durkheim (1970), for example, used suicide statistics, which he regarded as social facts, to investigate the causes of suicide.

Some sociologists admit that government statistics may be unreliable, but believe it is still possible to use them to produce reliable and valid data. For example, they believe that reliable crime statistics can be produced if surveys are conducted to supplement the information collected by the police.

Type of government crime statistics	How they are collected	Why they are useful	Main problems
Statistics on crimes known to the police	Police stations record events they believe to be criminal	Provides an estimate of the total number of crimes committed	Many crimes are not reported to the police Police have discretion in deciding which events to record
The British Crime Survey	Annual social survey using questionnaires to ask a sample of householders if they have been victims of crime	Provides an estimate of unreported crime	Respondents may not be truthful Interpretation is still required as to whether crime has taken place Sample may not be truly representative Not all crimes are included

Table 18
Government crime statistics

Interpretivist views of official statistics

From the interpretivist point of view, official statistics are not facts but merely an interpretation produced by government agencies. They argue that it is impossible to produce objective, reliable and valid statistics.

Interpretivists point out that all data requires classification and interpretation. For example, in crime statistics, the police, the Crown Prosecution Service and courts all have considerable discretion in determining whether a crime has taken place and whether a particular individual has committed the crime. To Cicourel (1976), the subjective classifications of police and courts makes this data invalid.

In another example, Maxwell Atkinson (1978) saw suicide statistics as the product of police and coroners' taken-for-granted assumptions about the sort of people who commit suicide.

Conclusion

- Some statistics may be relatively reliable and valid. For example, death statistics are highly reliable since the vast majority of deaths are likely to be recorded, and they are valid since it is easy to classify whether someone is alive or not.
- Some statistics are much less reliable and valid, such as crime statistics, because there is a large 'dark figure' of unrecorded crime and there is often considerable room for personal opinion in determining whether crime has taken place.
- Official statistics are nevertheless very useful, even if they are imperfect, because they are often the best available data on a topic.

Examiners' notes

In essay questions about official statistics, examine both viewpoints. This will allow you to score high marks for analysis and to introduce the evaluation that is needed to get into the top mark band.

Examiners' notes

Crime statistics are a useful example to illustrate the competing views on official statistics. The British Crime Survey is also a useful example to use in questions about surveys and questionnaire research.

Essential notes

Marxists argue that official statistics are distorted by the powerful (e.g. they believe governments define unemployment in such a way as to reduce the figures). Introduce this third perspective to gain more evaluation and analysis marks.

Examiners' notes

Always remember to include a short conclusion for 20-mark questions. Base it on the evidence and arguments put forward in your answer to show the examiner that you have thought about the issues and made a reasoned judgement about the question.

Qualitative secondary sources

Qualitative sources and documents

Qualitative sources are any sources with non-statistical content. They may be historical or contemporary and include:

- **public documents** – for example, transcripts of proceedings in Parliament, statements issued by companies
- **private documents** – for example, emails, paintings, song recordings, diaries and letters.

Historical sources

These are vital for studying long-term social changes.

- Max Weber (1958) used religious tracts to study the relationship between religious belief and the development of capitalism.
- Peter Laslett (1972, 1977) used parish records to show that **industrialization** led to an increase in extended family households in Britain.

However, a problem with all historical sources is that only a proportion will survive and there is no guarantee that they are **representative**. In particular, there tend to be few surviving documents produced by individuals, so that often the data that sociologists would like is not available. Also, qualitative sources reflect the subjective views of those who produced them. Nevertheless this is sometimes useful, as in Weber's work.

Life documents

Life documents are private documents created by individuals, which record subjective states. They include diaries, letters, photos, biographies, memoirs, suicide notes, films and pictures. Thomas and Znaniecki (1919) used letters and statements to study Polish peasants who emigrated to the USA.

Plummer (1982) argues that personal documents are rarely used by contemporary sociologists because:

- surviving documents may not be representative
- they are open to differing interpretations
- they are highly subjective – the same events discussed in a document such as a diary might be described very differently by someone else involved
- the content may be influenced by the identity of the person or people intended to read the document (except in documents intended to remain private).

However, Plummer believes that life documents are still very useful because:

- they allow insights into people's subjective states
- symbolic interactionists see them as revealing the personal meanings and self-concepts which they see as shaping behaviour.

The mass media and content analysis

The mass media may be unreliable for providing factual information, but some researchers see studies of the media as useful for revealing the ideological frameworks of those who produce it.

Content analysis (analysing the content of the media) tends to be a relatively cheap research method, and as media material is easily accessible there are few problems with **sampling** or **representativeness**.

There are various methods of content analysis:

Formal content analysis: content is classified and counted; for example, Best (1993) counted gender roles of boys and girls in children's books. It provides **objective** statistical data which **positivists** view as social facts, allowing patterns to be uncovered. However, classification of the data may be subjective and it does not directly reveal the meaning behind the content.

Thematic analysis: examines the message behind the portrayal of a particular topic; for example, Soothill and Walby (1991) studied rape coverage in newspapers. It makes it possible to look at the messages behind media coverage and reveal ideological bias. However, messages are open to alternative interpretations, and the audience may not interpret the content in the same way as researchers.

Textual analysis: involves detailed analysis of small pieces of text; for example, the Glasgow Media Group (1974) looked at the words used to describe managers and strikers. Textual analysis provides an in-depth interpretation of media content, but does not provide an overall analysis, and can be subjective.

Problems with qualitative sources

The points below summarize the problems with qualitative secondary sources as identified by John Scott (1990):

- **authenticity** – how genuine the documents are
- **soundness** – the document may be incomplete or unreliable
- **authorship** – it may not be written by the claimed author
- **credibility** – how believable the documents are
- **sincerity** – the author may have intended to mislead the readers
- **accuracy** – author may be untruthful
- **representativeness** – how typical the document is
- **survival**, or lack of it – representative documents may not exist
- **availability**, or lack of it – researchers may not be able to access representative samples
- **meaning** – how easy it is to understand the document
- **literal understanding** – it may be difficult to read or translate
- **interpretative understanding** – there may be possible different interpretations of what the document signifies.

The internet as a secondary source

Stuart Stein (2002) identifies particular problems in using the internet as a secondary source. There are often no editorial or review processes to ensure the validity of the data. Consequently, data needs to be used with caution.

Conclusion

Despite the above problems, qualitative secondary sources continue to be used because of their relative accessibility, cheapness and ability to produce insights into personal life and historical processes which could not otherwise be studied.

Essential notes

Several research projects by the Glasgow Media Group have found evidence that the UK news mass media tends to portray a pro-capitalist image of the world and to favour perspectives put forward by governments rather than by people opposed to government policies. In part this is because powerful groups are in a strong position to influence the news agenda and to have their views aired on television news.

Examiners' notes

The problems outlined in this list can be applied to any secondary source (statistical as well as qualitative). They can be used as the basis for the evaluation of secondary sources when answering essay questions. Remember to use examples from education.

Research in an educational context

The educational context

Research in education can involve the study of a variety of groups. These include:

- Educational staff such as teachers, head teachers and lecturers
- Pupils and students (the consumers of education)
- Parents of school pupils

Research may be conducted inside educational establishments, such as schools, colleges and universities, or outside those establishments, particularly when the research involves parents.

The general issues relating to research methods apply throughout; however, there are particular issues with researching in an educational context. The specific group being studied, and the context within which the study takes place, has an impact on the practical, ethical and theoretical aspects of conducting educational research.

1. Research into educational staff

Practical issues and educational staff research

- Access to educational staff may be limited by lack of time. Teachers may feel they have little time to commit to assisting with research.
- Schools are hierarchical institutions and teachers are only likely to take part in research with the permission of their line managers. This may restrict the availability of respondents.
- Senior educational staff are themselves subject to scrutiny; for example, headteachers are responsible to school governors. This may restrict their ability or willingness to take part in research.

Ethical issues and educational staff research

- Unguarded comments by educational staff could possibly affect career progression, so it is particularly important to maintain confidentiality for staff who take part in research.
- Observation of teachers within a staffroom setting has ethical problems if all members of the teaching staff have not consented to take part in the research.

Theoretical issues and educational staff research

- Teachers or lecturers are likely to associate the presence of an outsider in their classroom with Ofsted inspections and may act in untypical ways in order to impress the observer. This raises questions about the validity of classroom observations.
- In interview research there may be a degree of interviewer bias and teachers may give cautious answers rather than express their true opinions because they are concerned about confidentiality.
- The teaching staff put forward to take part in the research may be hand-picked by more senior staff in order to give a positive impression of the institution, making the findings unrepresentative.

2. Research into pupils and students
Practical issues and student research

- Researchers need to get approval for the research from parents and the school rather than just from the participants.
- The Department for Education or university governing body may also need to be approached for consent.
- In most circumstances researchers will need to undergo a Criminal Records Bureau check to ensure that they are suitable people to have close contact with children.
- Researchers also have to conform to the demands of the academic year so that the timing of their research is dependent on school, college or university terms, and avoiding key events such as exams.
- There are particular problems researching young pupils who may lack the skills or confidence to fill in questionnaires or answer complex questions. Research has to be designed to take account of the abilities of particular respondents and this may limit the range of information the researcher can collect.
- Researching young children can be particularly time-consuming as they have a tendency to stray from the central points of the research. This makes it potentially expensive.

Ethical issues and student research

There are specific ethical issues with studying children since they are considered particularly vulnerable.

- The researcher must ensure that children do not suffer any psychological distress during the research.
- Research could be interpreted as harming pupils and students if it distracts them from their education and therefore potentially impedes their performance.
- The British Sociological Association's guidelines state that the consent of children should be obtained as well as that of their parents. However, there are particular problems with gaining informed consent from young participants in research since they may not fully understand the purpose of the research.
- The guidelines also state that 'Researchers should have regard for issues of child protection and make provision for the potential disclosure of abuse'.

Theoretical issues and student research

Theoretical issues with research into the consumers of education partly depend upon their age.

- Educational consumers of all age-groups in schools, colleges and universities occupy relatively low-status positions. They have little power, which may make it difficult for them to openly express their views. This could affect the validity of their responses.
- There may be problems with young children expressing abstract ideas or understanding questions based upon those ideas, thereby making the validity of the data open to question.

Examiners' notes

The best answers will cover practical, ethical and theoretical issues. Think through the process of conducting research on the topic specified in the question and try to work out what the particular problems of doing that research might be.

This topic continues on the next two pages

Examiners' notes

To get high marks you must emphasize theoretical issues, as these will allow you to include more in-depth analysis and evaluation.

- In observation of classrooms, the presence of the observer may well produce unnatural behaviour.
- Since access to children is dependent upon the willingness of parents and teachers to allow researchers to question them, the representativeness of a sample could be compromised. This would make it difficult to generalize from the findings of the research.

3. Research into parents

Practical issues and parent research

Parents are not usually present in schools and other educational institutions. This makes it difficult to gain access for research purposes.

- There are practical data-protection issues in getting details of parental addresses and finding ways to approach them to secure their cooperation.
- Researching parents using interviews can be time-consuming, since each home will have to be visited separately at a time that is convenient to the parents, who may well be working during the day.
- Researchers are unlikely to be able to observe the behaviour of parents when they are discussing education with their children or assisting them with homework, since this takes place in private family settings, which are not accessible to researchers.

Ethical issues and parent research

Researching parents is much less ethically problematic than researching pupils, since parents can give properly informed consent.

The general ethical issues concerning research still apply, such as the problem of maintaining confidentiality.

Theoretical issues and parent research

There are particular problems in obtaining a representative sample of parents.

- Parents who may be more willing to take part in research than others will tend to be those who are more involved with their children's education. Therefore research data might exaggerate the degree to which parents assist children with homework or take an interest in their schooling.
- If questionnaires are used, then there may be an uneven response-rate from different groups of parents affecting the representativeness of the data.
- Parents may also feel that they need to create a good impression to the researcher by appearing actively interested in their children's schooling and homework. This may affect the validity of any responses.

Examiners' notes

The best answers will discuss both the strengths and the limitations of a particular method for studying an educational topic. It may be that the data produced is likely to be quite reliable but not very valid, or vice versa. This may give you a way of structuring your conclusion.

Examiners' notes

Making links between sociological theories, methodology and educational research can give your answer an extra level of sophistication, which will impress the examiner.

The influence of perspectives on educational research

Although practical and ethical issues have a strong impact on the type of educational research that is carried out, **table 19** shows how the theoretical perspective of the sociologist is also influential.

Perspective	Focus of research and example	Main advantages	Main problems
Functionalist	The positive contribution of education to society Example: Parsons (1961) on the functions of education	Relates education to the wider social structure	Based on abstract reasoning and not backed up by empirical evidence
Marxist/neo-Marxist	The way in which education serves the interests of ruling classes Example: Bowles and Gintis (1976) studied the hidden curriculum in the USA using questionnaire research. Paul Willis (1977) studied anti-school subculture using observation and interviews	Highlights educational inequality in the context of social structure and wider inequality Uses variety of methods to reveal this	Tends to emphasize class inequalities to the exclusion of other types (e.g. gender and ethnicity)
Social democratic	Class disadvantage in the education system Example: Halsey's (1977) statistical research into class differences in achievement	Provides evidence for changes in the education system (introduction of comprehensives). Relies largely on official statistics	Tends to have a narrow focus and neglects gender and ethnicity
Feminist	Patriarchal power and the education system Example: Stanworth's (1987) research into patriarchal power and sexism in a sixth form using interviews	Moves beyond concentration on class inequality and demonstrates the existence of sexism in education	May be dated, as doesn't take account of girls overtaking boys in the education system Whatever method is used, tends to have a narrow focus
Interpretivist	Classroom interaction, self-concepts, labelling and subcultures Example: Mac an Ghaill's (1994) study of boy's subcultures in secondary schools using participant observation and interviews	Based on direct observation of actual behaviour in schools and helps to reveal the meaning of schooling for those involved High on validity	Most interpretivist studies based on the subjective interpretations of researchers and neglect the wider social structure Low on reliability

Table 19
Influence of perspectives on educational research

The theoretical approach affects the type of data collected. Generally, structural approaches such as functionalism and Marxism tend to rely more on secondary sources for a wider analysis of the role of education in society. Interpretivists and feminists focus more on organization and processes within schools. Positivists favour quantitative methods such as questionnaires and using official statistics as secondary sources.

Essential notes

There are exceptions to this general correlation between perspectives and focus – some structural approaches try to link processes inside and outside schools; for example, Paul Willis' 1977 study of the anti-school subculture (see pp 8–9).

Examiners' notes

Only a few topics have
been studied using the
experimental method in
education, so it is a good bet
that any applied question
on experiments will ask
you about issues related to
labelling.

Essential notes

This research is ethically
controversial. Elliott
defended it as allowing
children to experience the
emotions associated with
racism so that it helped
to educate them against
being racist. However, the
research created divisions
and traumatized the children
in a way, which others would
consider unethical.

Experiments and questionnaire research in education
Experimental research in education

Experimental research into the education system has been limited.
However, there have been several high-profile research experiments
concerned with labelling theories of education and the effects of teachers'
expectations on pupil performance.

- Rosenthal and Jacobson (1968) gave false information to primary
  school teachers in the USA about the IQ of pupils. They found that
  regardless of what a pupil's actual IQ was, those who were believed
  by teachers to have a high IQ made greater progress than those who
  were believed to have a low IQ. This suggested that the self-fulfilling
  prophecy was occurring.
- Harvey and Slatin (1976) used photographs of children from
  different social classes and asked teachers to rate their likely
  performance in education. Pupils from higher classes were seen as
  more likely to be successful than pupils from lower social classes,
  suggesting that labelling on the basis of appearance does take place.

Key study
Jane Elliott: An experiment in discrimination

Jane Elliott, a primary school teacher in Iowa in the USA, conducted
an experiment in 1968 in which she deliberately discriminated in her
classroom. On the first day of the experiment, she told brown-eyed
children that they were inferior to blue-eyed children. She gave the
blue-eyed children extra playtime, and lots of positive feedback and
encouragement while the behaviour of the brown-eyed children was
persistently interpreted negatively and punished. On the second day,
the discrimination was reversed so that the brown-eyed children
were favoured. Whichever group of children was positively labelled
on a particular day, they performed much better on tests in class, and
visibly displayed much more enthusiasm for schooling. The experiment
led to temporary feelings of hostility between the two groups of
children.

Issues with experimental research in education
Practical issues and experimental research

Laboratory experiments are very difficult to conduct because of the
problems in gaining permission to conduct experiments and take children
out of the school environment. These formal types of experiments are
usually confined to studying older students rather than young children.

- The research by Harvey and Slatin was a type of laboratory
  experiment but was conducted on teachers rather than pupils.
- Field experiments such as those by Rosenthal and Jacobson
  and Elliott are more practical, but it may still be difficult to get
  permission from schools and teachers.

Ethical issues and experimental research

There are major ethical problems in conducting the types of experiments
described above, particularly if they involve school pupils. The research by

Rosenthal and Jacobson may have damaged the educational progress of some pupils who were labelled as having low ability. The research by Elliott led to divisions between the children within the school. In neither case was informed consent possible.

Theoretical issues and experimental research

Experiments, which by their very nature involve the creation of artificial situations, can lack validity. Attempts to reproduce the Rosenthal and Jacobson study have produced inconsistent results, suggesting that such research may not be very reliable.

Questionnaire research in education

Questionnaire research has been used in a wide variety of contexts, including the impact of parental attitudes to achievement (J.W.B. Douglas, 1964), the impact of **class** on cultural capital and achievement (Sullivan, 2001) and the choice of higher educational institution (Reay et al., 2005).

Key study

Alice Sullivan: Class, cultural capital and achievement

Alice Sullivan (2001) collected data from 465 pupils in four schools, using questionnaires. She asked questions about: parents' educational qualifications, the involvement of the children in cultural activities (for example, reading books, attending the theatre and concerts) and their own educational achievements. Sullivan found a link between the performance in GCSEs and having high levels of cultural capital. She also found that cultural capital was strongly linked to class background. Her conclusion was that parental income helps to boost the educational performance of children independent of cultural factors.

Practical issues and questionnaire research

Questionnaires make it possible to gather large amounts of information quickly and cheaply in educational settings. This type of research is relatively easy to conduct because of the existence of **sampling frames** such as lists of pupils and staff. It is also relatively easy to access large numbers of suitable respondents concentrated in one place. However, researchers are limited in the questions that they can put to young children or others with poor literacy skills.

Ethical issues and questionnaire research

The main ethical problem is maintaining anonymity of respondents. There may also be a problem with getting truly informed consent from young children.

Theoretical issues and questionnaire research

The dominance of **peer groups** may influence the types of answers that pupils give.

It might be difficult to prevent discussion among pupils so that they may end up collaborating on the responses. Children may be prone to making up misleading answers. This can undermine the validity of questionnaire findings.

Examiners' notes

Don't forget to mention some advantages of this type of research as well. For example, the research is easy to replicate, making it relatively easy for other researchers to check Rosenthal and Jacobson's findings. However, as the results have been mixed, it is difficult to reach definite conclusions.

Examiners' notes

This research is also useful for answering questions on differential achievement and social class. Remember that studies can be used both in the context of methodology questions and questions on education.

Essential notes

Questionnaires can be distributed to a large number of schools, giving a larger sample. By contrast, observational research or interviews are limited to one school at a time.

Interviews and participant observation

The use of interviews

Interviews have been used to study a wide range of educational topics. For example:

- Paul Willis (1977) used group interviews with the 'lads' who formed an anti-school subculture to understand their attitudes towards school, other pupils, teachers and careers.
- Stephen Frosh et al. (2002) used interviews with 78 boys in secondary school to collect data on their attitudes towards masculinity and how this affected their educational progress.

Key study

Willam Labov: Linguistic ability

William Labov (1973) used interviews with young black American children to investigate whether children from disadvantaged backgrounds had poor language skills. In the first set of interviews they were asked questions in a formal setting by a white interviewer. In the second set they were interviewed in a formal setting by a black interviewer, and in the third, in an informal setting, by a black interviewer. In the third setting the children were able to talk fluently, whereas in the first two their language was stilted.

Practical issues and interviews

- Interviewing children in schools requires consent from head-teachers and parents. This may limit access and those in authority may wish to restrict the scope of the interview.
- Interviewers may also be required to undergo a Criminal Records Bureau check.
- Interviews need to be carefully designed to take into account children's less developed language skills and shorter attention span. Questions therefore need to be phrased in simple language and the interview should be kept short.

However, interviews are a practical research method and it is possible to question children on a very wide range of subjects.

Ethical issues and interviews

- Interviews with children must be carefully designed so that they do not cause distress or fatigue. They should therefore be short and avoid issues that may be sensitive.
- The confidentiality of interviews needs to be assured, although if the interview reveals evidence of abuse, interviewers have a duty to report it, thus compromising confidentiality.

Theoretical issues and interviews

- As the study by Labov demonstrates, the validity of interview responses may be affected by the way in which the interview is conducted and by interviewer bias.
- Interviewees may see the interviewer as an authority figure, like a teacher or school inspector, and therefore be unwilling to give full and frank answers.

- Group interviews risk the responses being influenced by peer group pressure, although they may also be useful for drawing out the shared values of groups of pupils, which individuals might be reluctant to express (for example, Paul Willis's study).

Observation and participant observation
The uses of observational methods
Observational methods have been used widely in studying education, particularly non-participant observation. Some sociologists have conducted structured observation using the Flanders Interaction Analysis Categories (FIAC), which classify interaction in classrooms into one of 10 types and allow researchers to time the frequency and length of different types of interaction. Most observation is carried out in a less structured way; for example David Hargreaves (1967) observed teachers and pupils in secondary school without using a formal structure.

Key study

Devine: Observational research with primary-school children

Devine (2003) observed classrooms and playgrounds in three primary schools in Ireland. She made sure that she sat at desks with the children and never reported misbehaviour. She stayed in the playgrounds during breaks and avoided mixing too much with teachers so that she could better understand the schools from the children's point of view.

Practical issues in participant observation and observation
Issues of access can result from the need to obtain permission to carry out research. The role of the observer is problematic in schools, since the researcher is likely to be older than the children being observed. Observational research is likely to be time-consuming and therefore expensive, and there are practical issues about when and how field notes are recorded. Structured observation, however, makes it easier to record large amounts of standardized data.

Ethical issues in participant observation and observation
Covert observation by adults of children is unlikely to be seen as ethically acceptable. Researchers may face ethical dilemmas if they become aware of rule-breaking behaviour by children, and they may have to put confidentiality above disclosure. If such behaviour is discussed in the research report, it is important to guarantee anonymity in the research report.

Theoretical issues in participant observation and observation
The validity of observational research in education may be compromised by the **Hawthorne effect**. It may be impossible for researchers to blend into the background. Teachers and pupils may act unnaturally with the observer present; and the characteristics of the researcher, such as their age or ethnic group, might affect the results.

However, observation could be seen as more valid than other methods since it involves actual behaviour in real social settings.

Examiners' notes
Make your own additional notes on any examples of research using interviews. Examiners will be impressed if you are familiar with studies using the specified method on the particular topic.

Essential notes
When Hargreaves talked to some of the pupils, they told him that their teachers acted quite differently from normal when they were being observed.

Examiners' notes
Discussing theoretical issues is particularly important for scoring high marks.

Essential notes
Studies that rely mainly on unstructured observation or participant observation tend to reflect the interpretivist approach to research methods.

Secondary sources and education

The use of official statistics

Official statistics are very widely used in the study of education, particularly statistics about levels of attainment and subject choice. Statistics on truancy and school exclusions as well as transitions to work and higher education are also used in educational research. These statistics are particularly useful for examining longer-term trends and making comparisons between social groups.

Key study

Modood: Ethnicity, class and attainment

In a study of the relationship between ethnicity, **class** and attainment, Modood (2004) examined data on the proportion of pupils achieving five or more GCSE at grades A*–C in different ethnic groups. He examined data on pupils who were eligible for free school meals, and therefore from low-income families, with data on those who were not eligible. This enabled him to review the effects of income and ethnicity on achievement. He found that in all ethnic groups, pupils eligible for free school meals did less well than those who were not, but the effects of having a lower-income were much greater for white British pupils than other ethnic groups.

Practical issues and official statistics

Official statistics are an easily accessible and plentiful source of information on education. However, the information required by sociological researchers is not always available.

Data on achievement is usually broken down into the performance of males and females, but data on class backgrounds or the ethnicity of pupils and their achievement is less often available.

Official statistics do not always use the categories that sociologists use. For example, official definitions of social class do not always match sociological definitions, so sociologists sometimes have to use indirect indicators of class (such as eligibility for free school meals).

Ethical issues and official statistics

There are no real ethical issues in using official statistics, since they are publicly available and using them is unlikely to cause harm.

Theoretical issues and official statistics

Official statistics tend to be comprehensive, since it is often mandatory for state-funded organizations to produce them; they are also generally reliable since the government imposes definitions and categories on educational institutions and stipulates that data is produced using standardized procedures.

However, the validity of statistics may be open to question. For example, schools may deliberately manipulate data in order to secure funding, a favourable inspection report or success in league tables. Two examples of

Examiners' notes

Always relate your comments to the specific area of education highlighted in the question. Differential achievement, gender and subject choice and issues such as school attendance, exclusions or truancy might feature.

Essential notes

Where particular statistics are not produced as a matter of course, then sociologists have to rely on occasional survey research carried out by the government or other bodies. For example, data on ethnicity tends to be taken from the Youth Cohort Study. This makes comparisons over time more difficult, and because the data is based on a sample it is not as reliable as data produced by every school.

Essential notes

School league tables are a particularly contentious issue. The Labour government introduced Contextual Value Added (CVA) tables to take into account the background of pupils when judging school performance. However, the coalition government's White Paper of 2010 proposed the abolition of these types of league table.

this are when schools do not accurately record absences or lateness, or they exclude or fail to enter poorly performing pupils for exams to improve league-table performance.

Qualitative secondary sources in education

Sociologists can make use of a wide range of public documents relating to education. These include inspection reports, school policies and publicity brochures and the minutes of governors' meetings.

They also sometimes make use of personal documents such as written work, school reports on individual pupils, or notes passed in class.

Key study

Hey: Girls and friendship in education

Hey (2007) investigated friendship networks among girls in a secondary school using the notes that girls passed to one another during lessons. (She picked these notes out of the bin at the end of the lesson.) This allowed her to access the subjective views of girls, and build up a picture of their friendship networks, without using conventional methods such as interviews in which the honesty of the responses might be open to question.

Practical issues and qualitative secondary sources

Public documents tend to be easily available to researchers and are relatively cheap and quick to access, while personal documents are not available in such large quantities, nor are they necessarily easy to access, so relatively little research has been done using them.

Ethical issues and qualitative secondary sources

Public documents are already in the public domain, but when using private documents, ethical issues become more significant. The researcher may need to seek informed consent from those who produced the documents. If they fail to do so, then the research could be considered unethical (for example, Hey's picking private documents out of bins).

Some documents, such as school reports, could be considered to be confidential, and researchers should try to maintain the anonymity of pupils to whom they refer.

Theoretical issues and qualitative secondary sources

The validity of public documents may be open to question; some schools would not accept that inspection reports provide a valid assessment of the school.

School publicity material is likely to put a positive gloss on the school's image and performance, while documents produced for the government by schools may be manipulated to maximize funding or increase the likelihood of positive inspection reports.

Private documents have the potential to provide valid information on the subjective viewpoints of those involved in education. However, if they are intended to be read by someone else, they may be written in a way which has the audience in mind rather than being a completely valid account.

Essential notes

Quite a number of studies that use primary research methods supplement them with some analysis of documents. For example, in a study of the introduction of markets into education by Stephen Ball et al. (1994), extensive use was made of documents such as admissions policies and marketing material, as well as interviews with parents, in order to understand how the education market worked. Documents such as these can help a sociologist to understand the social policy context in which interaction takes place within schools.

Examiners' notes

Discuss the validity and reliability of sources in any questions on this topic. Use your general understanding of the theoretical issues surrounding secondary sources, and apply it to the particular educational topic you are asked to discuss.

General tips for the Education with Research Methods exam

The Education with Research Methods examination paper (SCLY2) consists of nine compulsory questions to be completed in two hours. The maximum mark for this paper is 90, so this is less than 1½ minutes per mark. There are 40 marks available for answering questions on the sociology of education, while 50 are for questions relating to research methods. You should not spend too long on the short questions that are at the start of each section. Answers to these should be clear and concise, as they are each worth only 2, 4 or 6 marks.

You will be given two Items to read to help you with some of the questions. Once you know what the questions are about, you should read the Items carefully to identify points or issues that you can use. Remember, the Items are there only to provide you with a starting point; this is NOT a comprehension.

- **Questions 01** and **06** are usually worth 2 marks and will ask you to explain a concept. You should give a clear explanation, not an example, and avoid using the term you are being asked about in your explanation. If there are inverted commas around the term to be explained, you should explain *all* the words *within* the inverted commas.
- **Questions 02, 07** and **08** will ask you to identify, suggest or explain two or three things. This could be two or three reasons, problems, criticisms, factors, effects, causes and so on. 'Identify' means that you need to state from your knowledge answers that are already established in sociology. 'Suggest' means that you can include any answer that you think might be appropriate or plausible. It's always a good idea to clearly separate the three points you are making – this makes your answer clearer for the examiner. Try not to choose answers that overlap. As with question 01 and 06, try to be concise – you will not earn extra marks for lots of detail or development that is not asked for. One sentence is often enough for each point.
- **Question 03** is an 'outline' question which is a sort of mini-essay. You will be asked to consider a narrower range of material than for the full essay questions. This is often shown by asking for 'some of' the ways, factors, and so on. This means you are not expected to try to cover the whole range of points available. Often three or four points well explained and analysed can earn more marks than a list of 10 points with minimal analysis. 8 of the 12 marks here are for knowledge and understanding. However, you still need to display some AO2 skills of interpretation, application, analysis and evaluation. You should analyse the points you are assembling, and suggest a few points of evaluation.
- **Question 04** is the essay question on education. It will usually ask you to use the Item and therefore you will not be able to gain top marks if you do not do so. You should try to build on the Item by developing some of the ideas put forward. However, the phrase 'and elsewhere' means that you are expected to contribute a lot of your own ideas – the Item will not provide everything you need. This question will usually ask you to 'assess'. Assessment involves

evaluation and judgement, so you must therefore make sure that you are analytical and evaluative in your answer. 12 of the 20 marks for this essay are for AO2 skills and only 8 marks are for AO1 knowledge and understanding skills. Make sure you include some references to the wording of the question, to sociological concepts and perspectives, and that you cover all the elements in the question.

- **Question 05** is the Methods in Context question. First of all, remember that this is a question about research methods 'in context'. You will be asked to choose one method to apply. Do not spend time talking about sociological views on the issue. You should show that you understand the strengths and weaknesses of the method in question, but the most important thing is to consider the application of the method to the particular issue being asked about. Consider who the subjects are – what are their research characteristics? What do you know about pupils or teachers that makes them different in some way to other subjects? What is special about a school or classroom that is different to a factory or office, for example? Then consider how these facts affect the way the method can be applied and how successful it might be. The more you can apply the strengths and weaknesses of the method to the particular group, situation and issue, the more marks you will gain. Think carefully about these issues before you decide which method to choose.

- **Question 09** is the essay question on research methods. This one will not have an Item to refer to but, like the education essay, will ask you to 'assess', so you should follow the instructions given above about assessment for the education essay. This question has 20 marks split equally between AO1 knowledge and understanding skills and AO2 interpretation, application, analysis and evaluation skills. Make sure you focus clearly on the question set. If you are asked about the advantages of something, you should focus on this rather than the disadvantages (although you may wish to include some of these as evaluation).

When writing each of the essays you should look back regularly to the question. Make sure you have obeyed all of the instructions and covered all of the issues included in the question. Some essays have two or more parts. You will not gain top marks if you do not deal with each part. It is also very important to focus on the question set. Do not be tempted to write an essay about all you know on the topic in question, or to spend time writing at a tangent to the question – try to use your material to focus on the issues.

Education with Research Methods (sample exam paper 1)

Education

Read Item A below and answer questions 01 to 04 that follow.

Item A

There are significant differences in educational achievement between different ethnic groups. Whereas the average achievement level of white children is close to the national average, that of Chinese pupils is significantly higher and that of black pupils is significantly lower.

One approach to these differences in educational achievement is to explain it as the result of cultural differences of language, socialization or family patterns.

Some sociologists argue that social class is the most important factor in educational achievement. However, a study produced by the University of London in 2010 found that the gap in achievement between working-class and middle-class pupils is far greater for white pupils than for other ethnic groups.

Questions

01 Explain what is meant by the term 'self-fulfilling prophecy'. [**2 marks**]

02 Suggest **three** reasons why some parents are better able than others to choose which school their child attends. [**6 marks**]

03 Outline the Marxist view of the role of education in legitimating inequality. [**12 marks**]

04 Using material from **Item A** and elsewhere, assess sociological explanations of ethnic differences in educational achievement. [**20 marks**]

Methods in Context

*This question requires you to **apply** your knowledge and understanding of sociological research methods to the study of this **particular** issue in **education**.*

Item B

Investigating pupils' career aspirations

According to some sociologists, many children start off their school lives with a wide range of ideas about what career they might take up as adults. However, as they progress through school, young people's aspirations often become more limited, as they come to terms with factors that may prevent them from realizing their goals.

Sociologists may use written questionnaires to investigate aspirations and the changes that may take place during a pupil's school years. Once permission from the schools has been granted, the researcher may have access to a range of pupils from different backgrounds. They can also ask precise questions about the factors they wish to study. However, pupils may not understand the way different groups or circumstances can influence their views. Questionnaires may not provide much detail about the way the pupils see their future.

Question

05 Using material from **Item B** and elsewhere, assess the strengths and limitations of using **written questionnaires** for investigating pupils' career aspirations. **[20 marks]**

Research Methods

*These questions permit you to draw examples from **any areas** of sociology with which you are familiar.*

Questions

06 Explain what is meant by the term 'pilot study'. **[2 marks]**

07 Suggest **one** advantage and **one** disadvantage of using historical documents in sociological research. **[4 marks]**

08 Identify **two** ethical issues that sociologists need to take into account when carrying out research. **[4 marks]**

09 Assess the usefulness of official statistics in sociological research. **[20 marks]**

Grade A answer

01 *Explain what is meant by the term 'self-fulfilling prophecy'.* [**2 marks**]

> A self-fulfilling prophecy is a predicted situation that becomes true, for example a teacher may expect something of a child and it becomes true because the child lives up to the teacher's expectation.

The concept has been correctly explained.
Mark 2/2

02 *Suggest* **three** *reasons why some parents are better able than others to choose which school their child attends.* [**6 marks**]

> Money is one factor that might mean parents are more able to find a suitable school for their child. For example, those with increased wealth are more able to enter their children for private schools, whereas those with a limited income are less able. Parental communication is another issue. If a parent lacks the communication and interest needed for finding a school, such as contacting teachers, attending open days and retrieving information, the child may be at a disadvantage. Finally, cultural capital also affects a parent's ability to choose a school.

Two appropriate reasons are suggested: sufficient income for private school; parental communication skills. The point about cultural capital is too similar. It is also useful to separate the three points more clearly for the examiner.

Other appropriate answers might include: ability to afford housing in the area; travel costs; number of choices available; language differences; children may be sought after by a school.
Mark 4/6

03 *Outline the Marxist view of the role of education in legitimating inequality.* [**12 marks**]

> Marxists believe that education performs two main roles. Firstly, reproducing class inequalities and the means of production that serve the capitalist system. Secondly, making this inequality look reasonable through the idea of meritocracy. This is what is meant by 'legitimating inequality'.
>
> Althusser is one Marxist that holds this view. He believes that education acts as an 'ideological state apparatus' that, first, reproduces the values of the capitalist system and controls people's ideas and values. He believes that education passes on ruling-class values to children in school and perpetuates inequalities through education. Then, secondly, it also justifies inequalities by persuading people in school that inequality is inevitable. Inequality is 'legitimated' by persuading people that those who do very well are the most talented.
>
> Bowles and Gintis also believe education acts in the same way. Their 'correspondence theory' argues that school operates like work, with a hierarchy of teachers that pupils have to obey, just like bosses and workers. This ensures the future workers accept the capitalist system and adapt to its needs. They argue that teachers act like bosses, encouraging students to work for rewards. They also argue that this happens through the 'hidden curriculum'. ☞

A good introductory paragraph. The terms of the question are explained.

An appropriate Marxist example is described and linked to the question, though the second, more important point is not explained fully.

A good explanation of the correspondence theory. This is linked to the question more closely in the next paragraph.

This means that many things are taught in schools that are not in the official rules and timetables, but are values and norms that are passed on to the pupils in the way things are done every day. Pupils learn about being at the bottom of a hierarchy, being obedient, and competing with each other, and this prepares them to be well-behaved workers in the future. This therefore supports capitalism and reproduces it.

Bowles and Gintis then go on to argue that education operates with a 'myth of meritocracy' where pupils blame themselves rather than the system if they don't do well. This is the way inequality is legitimated. They are taught that everyone has the same chance, and those who do well are the ones who are cleverest and work the hardest. So those who are successful are there because they deserve it. If you fail, it's because you haven't tried hard enough or you are not clever enough. So all the inequalities from school are 'legitimated'. Everyone sees it as fair that some end up with good jobs and very high incomes. But this is a myth – it hides the fact that your success in education is linked very closely to your social class, so people don't have the same chance at all. Bowles and Gintis also say that this even justifies the fact that some people are in poverty.

> Here the discussion of the work of Bowles and Gintis is focused much more closely on the question of legitimating inequality. There is some sound analysis shown.

Finally, Willis studied the 'lads' who were a group of working-class boys who found school was very boring and had an anti-school subculture. They didn't accept the myth of meritocracy – they didn't work hard and made fun of the boys who did. So this seems to conflict with Bowles and Gintis – the boys don't just accept the myth. But Willis argued that they still went the same way. Because they were rebels they still ended up in boring, unskilled jobs, so the school still prepared them for that anyway.

> Although this study appears to be contradicting the idea of legitimating inequality, the writer shows how it may be seen actually to support it. Good analysis and evaluation.

Overall this is a very good answer. There is a clear focus on Marxist views on the role of education in legitimating inequality. Several Marxist sources are referred to and a number of relevant sociological concepts used. There is good evidence of the skill of analysis and some evaluation.

The first paragraph about the work of Bowles and Gintis does not focus on the legitimating of inequality, but does put the concept in context. The focus could also be closer for the Althusser paragraph.

More evaluation could be supplied, by reference to criticisms that have been made of Bowles and Gintis or by reference to other perspectives, such as postmodernist, interactionist or feminist views.

Mark 10/12

---

04 *Using material from **Item A** and elsewhere, assess sociological explanations of ethnic differences in educational achievement.*
    [20 marks]

Ethnicity refers to a person's cultural background based on factors such as religion and language. Educational achievement means how well a student progresses in school and how well they do as a result. Ethnicity can be ☞

A good opening paragraph which explains terms, illustrates the differences to be considered and suggests that there may be a debate on this issue.

The issue of language is appropriately raised and an evaluative point made.

Other cultural factors, family structure and norms, are analysed and related to specific minority ethnic groups. A good evaluative point, relating lack of achievement to low income, is made. The suggestion that effects may be positive or negative is made.

Skills of analysis and evaluation are shown well in this paragraph, returning to the issue of low income and showing that it may be more important than ethnicity. Again, a specific group is given as an example.

A very good paragraph, illustrating a range of ways in which in-school factors may influence achievement. An alternative perspective is identified, supported by reference to sociological research.

seen to affect this through several ways such as the education system itself or cultural background. As Item A says, there are considerable differences in achievement. For example, a smaller percentage of black, Pakistani and Bangladeshi children gain five or more GCSEs than the white population, but Indian and Chinese do better. However some people argue that ethnicity is not the only factor to affect educational achievement.

One way that ethnicity may affect educational achievement is through cultural factors. As the Item says, this can refer to language differences in the home that create a barrier in communication. For example, a child is less likely to understand things at school if they find it difficult understanding the language. Ball adds to this by arguing that parents' language barriers mean that they are unable to have good communication with their child's school. However, this does not seem to affect the higher educational levels of Indian and Chinese children.

A pupil's family background can also affect educational achievement. One example of this is that African-Caribbean students are more likely to come from a background with a lone mother, in which case they arguably lack a father figure. This would be bad for their educational achievement because they may have no male role model at home. However, this may also be related to low income, rather than just ethnicity, because there is only one earner. Some sociologists have argued that Asian families are more likely to encourage their children to high achievement. Lupton says they also encourage respectful behaviour, which helps them to fit in with school. Therefore it is clear that a student's cultural background can have negative or positive effects for their educational achievement.

However, a pupil's ethnicity may also mean they come from different economic backgrounds. Item A says that social class is the most important factor in educational achievement. For example, Bangladeshi students tend to come from lower income backgrounds. This will have negative effects on a child's educational achievement because they have limited resources compared with other students. On the other hand, those that have lots of material goods may find this is beneficial in schools in order to make friends and be part of the 'crowd'. Material deprivation can therefore have negative effects for the pupil; so much of the difference between ethnic groups may be the effect of social class or low pay, not ethnicity. Marxist sociologists would see these social class differences as the most important ones.

Interactionist sociologists stress the importance of internal factors in education and the way interaction in the school can be seen to affect achievement. First, some of the curriculum is 'ethnocentric', oppressing ethnic minority groups by a focus on British culture and ignoring other cultures. For example, in history, bringing up issues like slavery and civilizing primitives, or only teaching European languages. This will affect a child's self-esteem and possibly their achievement. Coard argues that the system therefore ignores black students and does not allow them to experience the full advantages of education. Gillborn goes further by saying education is racist. This is because teachers create stereotypical assumptions about ethnic minority students, and give them ☞

less help. Ethnic minority students are more likely to be in the lower bands and teachers are seen to ignore these 'no hopers', meaning that for ethnic minority students it is harder to make progress. Black pupils are also more likely to be excluded from school and Gillborn believes that the fact that black pupils are more likely to be punished like this is due to fear by teachers.

However, there are two main reasons why these theories can be criticized. Some sociologists argue that ethnic differences are not so important in producing such differences in achievement. For example, Indian students tend to do very well in the education system – rather than be disadvantaged by it they do well and have high rates of university entrance. Sometimes a background such as poor income may motivate pupils to do well. The second criticism is that they ignore other factors such as class and gender. For example, black girls tend to do better in education than white boys. Postmodernists continue this by saying postmodern society and the differences that exist within a wide range of ethnic groups are too complex to generalize about the effects of ethnicity, gender or class.

In conclusion it is clear that achievement levels do differ depending on ethnicity, however it is questionable as to whether or not this is solely due to ethnic differences. In this case it can be argued that a closer look needs to be taken when looking at educational achievement.

Excellent evidence of the skill of evaluation. Four different points of evaluation are clearly explained.

A rather disappointing conclusion – a brief summary, saying very little. However, the points are well made elsewhere.

Overall this is a very good answer. It shows a good level of sociological knowledge and understanding. The answer includes consideration of both cultural and material differences outside school, plus the possible influence of several in-school factors. This shows good interpretation of the question, and good application of sociological knowledge. This is a complex question – it would be difficult to cover all the possible material in the time available, so the question of balance is important.

Throughout the answer there is evidence of analysis and evaluation. Concepts and ideas are explained and discussed and reference is made to several sociological perspectives. Material from the Item is used appropriately and there are several sociological sources used.

The temptation to lump all minority ethnic groups together is avoided. In many places the writer makes a point of differentiating between groups and showing that they have different experiences in education.

The answer is well organized and well-focused, though the conclusion is rather weak. Each element of the question has been addressed. However, the notion of 'ethnicity' is rather narrow, as there is little consideration of white pupils – i.e. the ethnic majority. There needs to be some consideration of white achievement, or lack of, to show that there is much research on this. Although the answer deals with cultural, material and in-school factors, it would be useful to look at the interrelations between these.

Mark 17/20

Methods in Context

05 *Using material from **Item B** and elsewhere, assess the strengths and limitations of using written questionnaires for investigating pupils' career aspirations.* **[20 marks]**

A reasonable first paragraph, pointing to some strengths of the method, but these are not applied to the question – they could be applied to any topic or any group being studied.

Some strengths and weaknesses of the method with a weak link to the issue (though this is linked later in the answer).

Another strength of the method is mentioned and linked to theory and ethical issues. There is an attempt to link to pupils.

A relevant research characteristic of the pupils is explained.

This is a very good paragraph, well focused on the elements of the question. Another research characteristic is explained, this is related to the completion of questionnaires and also to the measurement of aspirations.

There are clearly some advantages to using written questionnaires when researching pupil's career aspirations – they can be high in reliability and provide good statistical data, while ensuring that each pupil is asked exactly the same questions in exactly the same way. So therefore the findings are high in reliability and the method could be used by another researcher to repeat and check the findings. This also means that there is no possible interviewer bias.

One strength of using written questionnaires is that, as Item B says, once the researcher has gained access from the gatekeeper they can interview a 'range of pupils from different backgrounds', thus allowing them to gain the experiences of pupils across many different ethnic and social class backgrounds, which in turn gives their research more generalizibility and representativeness. This is especially useful given that many sociologists believe that these issues are directly linked to educational achievement, which will affect their chances of achieving in their preferred career: using these questionnaires could prove invaluable in proving or disproving this theory. Because the questionnaires have set, unchanging questions, which are often pre-coded, the need for lengthy training of research staff is much less than for other methods.

Another strength of using written questionnaires is that they provide good statistical data. Due to their format, it is easy for sociologists to collect data which they can publish in a statistical format. For positivists, this increases the credibility of a piece of research, something impossible if one used only focus groups or participant observation. However, interpretivists argue that they don't allow people to say things in their own way; due to the set questions pupils may be restricted from including vital pieces of data and there may also be ethical problems, as pupils, realizing that certain careers may be beyond them, could be upset.

Because the participants are pupils, who have less power and status in the school, they may see the researcher as an authority figure, which could affect the way they complete their answers. They might try to give what they thought was the 'right answer', or they might lie.

You would also need to take account of the possible influence of peer group pressure. If the questions are completed in class, there would have to be strict supervision to ensure that the pupils didn't affect each other's answers. Research on peer groups shows that kids are often made fun of if they are too keen to do well, so answers on their aspirations might be particularly affected by this. Similarly, in a pro-school peer group, those with low aspirations might be laughed at. However, if supervised properly, this could be avoided with written questionnaires, whereas it couldn't be with some forms of interviews.

Item B highlights that the researcher requires 'permission from the schools', with the teachers being 'gatekeepers' in this particular instance. Thus there is always a chance that the school may reject the sociologist's request for ☞

the study, preferring to protect their students from such questioning because they are vulnerable. It might also be necessary to get consent from parents.

However, once you had consent, this could be very useful and ensure that there was a very high response rate, because the kids had to do what the head said. This provides good representativeness. Response rates are often a big problem with questionnaires. On the other hand, many teachers and heads would not want any disruption to their lessons, but the pupils would not want to lose their free time. If they took the questions home, they would not be as valid, because the parents might fill them in for them.

It would be very important to take into account the fact that you are questioning pupils. The Item points out that you could look at children at different stages, so their understanding and reading skills might be limited, and also their vocabulary. So questioning young pupils would probably make writing the questions difficult. Pupil aspirations are a complex topic to put into questions; it's important not to over-simplify the questions, because this would not produce appropriate answers. On the other hand, young children may not have very good concentration, so it must not be too long.

Another reason the answers might not be wholly true is because the sociologist may give pupils ideas about careers that the pupil would not otherwise have. Pupils may not have thought about their aspirations until they were asked to do so. By raising the issue of whether certain careers are open only to certain students the sociologist may dissuade the pupils from attempting to pursue a certain career. This obviously has ethical implications.

An additional research characteristic is explained, but not linked to the use of questionnaires.

The strengths and weaknesses of questionnaires are linked in several ways to the characteristics of schools.

A good paragraph on the particular characteristics of pupils. This is linked well to the use of written questions on aspirations.

Some further points about studying aspirations, but not specifically related to the use of questionnaires.

This is a very good answer that deals with the issues raised by the question. A number of strengths and weaknesses of written questionnaires are discussed. Most importantly, the use of this method is considered with regard to the particular issue of studying pupil career aspirations. However, these two aspects could have been woven together, rather than dealt with separately.

Interpretation and application are therefore good. Analysis and evaluation are explicit and relevant. The research characteristics of pupils and the school setting have been appropriately analysed.
Mark: 17/20

Research Methods

06 *Explain what is meant by the term 'pilot study'.* [**2 marks**]

A pilot study is a small-scale trial of research that is carried out prior to the main research. This is important in highlighting any unforeseen problems or inaccuracies.

A very good answer. The term has been correctly explained.
Mark 2/2

07 *Suggest **one** advantage and **one** disadvantage of using historical documents in sociological research.* **[4 marks]**

> One advantage of using historical documents is that if the sociologist is researching something in the past there may be no one to interview or study, for example war victims may have passed away. Therefore the historical document provides information that isn't otherwise available. However one disadvantage is that the sociologist may be unaware as to whether or not the document is free from error such as low validity, reliability or representativeness which will in turn affect their research.

One appropriate advantage and one appropriate disadvantage have been identified. It would be useful to present the examiner with these two points clearly separated in different paragraphs.

Other advantages might be that the documents are readily available and cheap to access.

Other disadvantages might be that they may not be authentic, credible or the precise meaning may be difficult to decipher.
Mark 4/4

08 *Identify **two** ethical issues that sociologists need to take into account when carrying out research.* **[4 marks]**

> One possible ethical issue that sociologists need to be aware of when conducting research is that some issues can be very sensitive for participants, and need to be approached very carefully (if at all). For example, if looking into why people commit suicide, one would have to be very careful when interviewing relatives of the deceased: discussion of such a tragic topic would likely bring back dark memories which the participants would rather forget.
>
> Another ethical issue to consider when conducting research is the age of the participant. If researching young children, for instance, the sociologist must ensure they have gained the necessary consent from the gatekeeper (in this case probably the parent), as well as from the child themselves: failure to do so would be highly unethical because young children are vulnerable.

Two appropriate issues are identified: sensitivity (and potential harmful effect); and children as a vulnerable group. However, less detail is needed.

Other possible answers might include: confidentiality; privacy; danger; legality; informed consent.
Mark 4/4

09 *Assess the usefulness of official statistics in sociological research.*
    [20 marks]

> Official statistics are data collected by the government and other organizations that are used for specific purposes. For example official statistics are used to measure crime and deviance in the country. Usefulness refers to the validity, representativeness and reliability of the data collected. As quantitative data, it is likely to be high in representativeness and reliability while low on validity in regards to depth. However, their usefulness for sociologists in their research may vary considerably. ☞

A reasonably good introduction, explaining the meaning of official statistics and referring to their potential usefulness.

There are many advantages for sociologists in using official statistics. For example they are collected by the government which means the figures are often readily available for sociologists to use. This has a positive effect of saving time and money, therefore showing official statistics to be a practical method. It also means that data is reliable as statistics carried out by the government are likely to be very accurate and can be repeated many times. Representativeness is also high when using official statistics as they provide data from a widespread area, covering a greater scale than sociologists would ever be able to achieve and therefore generalizations can be made to the whole population. All of these characteristics mean that the sociologist has available material on a very large scale that they could not possibly gather themselves. Statistics are collected over a very wide range of subjects indeed, including the whole census every 10 years.

Official statistics are collected regularly so they provide a historical overview which means that trends and patterns can be shown. This also means that comparisons can be made, for example it's possible to look at figures for crime before and after the law has been changed. Finally official statistics do not involve any of the ethical problems faced in other research methods.

Positivist sociologists see statistics as a valuable source of quantitative data. They take the statistics at face value (as objective facts) and are able to build theories based on them. For example, Durkheim built his theory of suicide on statistics from all over Europe. He compared different groups and regions to see the patterns, such as religion and marriage, and how these related to suicide rates. However, interpretive sociologists do not accept statistics at face value – they argue that statistics are produced by individual decisions and are 'socially constructed'. For example, a crime is not a crime unless it has been found out and labelled as a crime by the police. So the statistics are not a valid measure of crime because they do not measure what they are meant to be measuring.

There are also many disadvantages to using official statistics. One disadvantage of using official statistics is that they are often created for government purposes, and may omit information the sociologist may need. This lowers the usefulness of official statistics because information that is important to the sociologist's research may be missing. The statistics may also be affected by political considerations, which means the government may be intent on making the figures look positive, so may leave out questions they don't want asking, or alter the way something like unemployment is measured to make the figures look smaller. This has the effect of creating inaccurate data, which is not reliable or valid, therefore lowering its usefulness.

There are also statistics that are not provided by the government, for example NGOs, businesses and pressure groups. These are useful in providing a large amount of information but these bodies are less powerful than the government. This may affect the usefulness of the data as it may not be as representative. However these organizations are also likely to try to make their data positive, so sociologists are often reluctant to depend on it. This lowers the usefulness of the data as it may not be very reliable or valid. These are often referred to as 'soft' statistics, because they can be manipulated, but this can also be 👉

A good paragraph that provides a list of practical strengths of the method, with some analysis at the end. However, references to reliability and validity are not very clear.

Two further appropriate practical strengths of the method are outlined, with an example. There is a brief mention of the ethical dimension.

Here, the views of two sociological perspectives on official statistics are applied correctly and illustrated with appropriate examples.

Two practical weaknesses of the method are analysed. An opportunity is missed here to provide a link from political considerations to Marxist views about official statistics and the way they may be used to maintain the power of the capitalist class.

The answer here correctly includes non-governmental statistics that might be used by sociologists, and briefly explains why they may be less representative. 'Soft and 'hard' statistics are correctly differentiated.

applied to some government statistics; for example, unemployment or waiting lists. Sociologists can rely much more on 'hard' statistics. These are the counts of things like births and deaths, which are not manipulated.

In conclusion the usefulness of official statistics very much depends on where they come from and what they were designed for. However they can be useful in sociological research where a sociologist is aware of the vested interest that may be present. Additionally perspectives such as realists and functionalists are positive towards official statistics, highlighting that they do have some degree of usefulness.

A good conclusion that refers back to the wording of the question and summarizes the main points.

This is a good answer that covers both practical and theoretical issues. Both the potential strengths and weaknesses of the method are analysed. There is also a brief reference to ethical issues. Specific examples are provided for some of the points made – this might usefully be done more often. The writer tries to focus on the question of 'usefulness'.

However, the focus is mainly on practical issues, although positivist and interpretive approaches to official statistics are analysed and juxtaposed in evaluation. The answer could be improved by extending this discussion to include Marxist and feminist views. The explanation of 'hard' and 'soft' statistics could also be more focused – it seems to be rather an afterthought.

A number of sociological concepts are correctly used.
Mark 16/20

Total marks: 2 + 4 + 10 + 17 + 17 + 2 + 4 + 4 + 16 = 76/90 = Grade A

Education with Research Methods (sample exam paper 2)

Education

Read Item A below and answer questions 01 to 04 that follow.

Item A

Many sociologists argue that there is a clear link between educational achievement and material factors in a child's home background, such as low income and poor housing. A common measure of child poverty is whether or not a child receives free school meals; this correlates closely with weak examination results. Lack of sufficient financial support may have an impact on many aspects of a child's experience at school and on the opportunities available to that child beyond school.

Another approach suggests that cultural differences, such as socialization or family structure, may be more important than material deprivation.

Questions

01 Explain what is meant by the term 'cultural capital'. [**2 marks**]

02 Suggest **three** ways in which schooling in a capitalist society may mirror the features of the workplace. [**6 marks**]

03 Outline some of the factors involved in the development of pupil subcultures. [**12 marks**]

04 Using material from **Item A** and elsewhere, assess the extent to which material deprivation is the most important home factor in affecting social class differences in educational achievement. [**20 marks**]

Methods in Context

*This question requires you to **apply** your knowledge and understanding of sociological research methods to the study of this **particular** issue in **education**.*

Read Item B below and answer question 05 that follows.

Investigating teacher expectations of pupils' educational achievement

Some sociologists claim that teachers hold views about individual pupils and how well they expect those pupils to succeed in education. There are many factors both inside and outside the school that may contribute to the formation of these expectations. Once established, these expectations may affect the way in which the teacher deals with a pupil and how much time and effort is spent on that pupil.

Sociologists may use participant observation to study teacher expectations, by observing their interaction with pupils in the classroom. This has the advantage of the researcher's seeing how teachers actually treat their pupils and how the pupils respond. Researchers might also measure the effect of other teachers' opinions, by observing interactions in the staffroom.

However, there may be problems in using this method because both the classroom and the staffroom are relatively 'closed' social settings.

Question

05 Using material from **Item B** and elsewhere, assess the strengths and limitations of using **participant observation** for investigating teacher expectations of pupils' educational achievement. [**20 marks**]

Research Methods

*These questions permit you to draw examples from **any areas** of sociology with which you are familiar.*

Questions

06 Explain what is meant by a 'representative sample'. [**2 marks**]

07 Suggest **two** reasons why a researcher may choose to use structured rather than unstructured interviews. [**4 marks**]

08 Identify **two** practical reasons for using postal questionnaires. [**4 marks**]

09 Examine the usefulness of different forms of qualitative secondary sources in sociological research. [**20 marks**]

Grade C answer

01 *Explain what is meant by the term 'cultural capital'.* **[2 marks]**

> Cultural capital refers to the advantage that some children have (usually those of middle- or upper-class backgrounds) when it comes to education. They have these advantages essentially because their parents have more time to prepare them for the schooling experience, giving them an upper hand over the working class and hence making them more suited to achieve well in education.

This is only a partially satisfactory explanation. The answer refers to the way in which middle-class parents pass on advantage to their children. This is correct. However, 'cultural capital' is not about having more time available, but refers to what is passed on, such as middle-class values, knowledge or language – all of which may give advantage.

Mark 1/2

02 *Suggest **three** ways in which schooling in a capitalist society may mirror the features of the workplace.* **[6 marks]**

> Mac an Ghaill found boys in schools pick on those who don't conform to the stereotype of 'hegemonic masculinity', and this also occurs in the workplace (particularly manual work), with physical strength being a key factor and seen as very desirable. Putting in too much effort is also frowned upon by peers both at school and at work.
>
> Secondly, in both the workplace and at school the middle and upper class have an advantage. French sociologist Pierre Bourdieu coined the phrase 'cultural capital', and it would certainly appear to be that the working class are invariably at a disadvantage.
>
> Finally, at school, children are taught that they must do as they are told by those in charge and must work hard. This prepares them for the workplace, where they are expected to do the same by the bosses.

Two appropriate features are suggested: the effects of peer group pressure and the hierarchy of authority. However, the second example does not score: it is not a specific feature of the workplace, unless it could be related to selection and promotion.

A more appropriate answer to this question would use several of the features held in common by schools and work that are identified by Bowles and Gintis in the 'correspondence principle' – such as fragmentation of work; extrinsic rewards; competition; **alienation**; hierarchy of authority. The question ('schooling in a capitalist society') in fact suggests that a Marxist approach might provide a good answer.

Mark 4/6

03 *Outline some of the factors involved in the development of pupil subcultures.* **[12 marks]**

One factor involved in the development of pupil subcultures is the role played by teachers. Teachers might have different attitudes towards different pupils based on their family situation, reports from previous schools and criminal records. As such, pupils can become 'labelled' as good or bad, and may as a result conform to the stereotype expected of them by forming a subculture (e.g. those who underachieve are more likely to hang out with other low achievers, whereas those who succeed are more likely to be pushed towards academic activities and thus will associate themselves with other 'clever' pupils).

Another factor is the part played by peer groups, who have a massive influence over individuals. Some may feel socially compelled to conform to the pressure they are put under by peers, perhaps due to a fear of being branded a swot. Haywood found in his study that clever students were often branded as 'bum bandits' or 'wankers', which would seem to suggest that success at school is often perceived as uncool (although it seems to become more acceptable the higher up the educational ladder you go).

Finally, the role played by parents may also influence pupil subcultures. Frank Furedi's study on 'paranoid parents' represents the growing fear for many that their children are at risk from strangers, and thus they may be more inclined to carefully monitor whom they spend their time with, cutting out those whom they deem as unsuitable. Since kids spent a lot of their time at school, this may lead particularly to middle-class parents attempting to find suitable friends at clubs and activities, fearing their children might underachieve if they didn't find similar academic peers for their kids.

A good paragraph. Stereotyping and labelling by teachers are identified as reasons. Both of these are explained and there is some analysis of the way they may lead to the formation of subcultures. Both deviant and academic subcultures are mentioned.

Another reason, the pressure of peer groups, is identified and further explained. This is supported by evidence and a brief evaluative point is made at the end.

A further reason is identified, supported by evidence and analysed. The focus here is on pro- rather than anti-school pupils, though the link to subculture development is weaker.

Overall this is a reasonable answer. Four possible reasons are identified and discussed. There are some sociological concepts and some evidence from research. The skills of analysis and evaluation are evident to some degree.

However, the range of material is somewhat limited. Other concepts that might be used include streaming, differentiation, polarization, retreatism, racism, gender, social class etc.

Mark 7/12

04 *Using material from **Item A** and elsewhere, assess the extent to which material deprivation is the most important home factor in affecting social class differences in educational achievement.* **[20 marks]**

There is certainly evidence to suggest that household income is the key determinant in educational achievement – as Item A says, those who receive free school meals (an indication of low income) invariably do worse in education. Further, this lack of income may be important in an individual's decision to go on to higher education – those with financial problems may ☞

A good paragraph that identifies the importance of income levels in application to higher education and shows the importance of both family and peer group. An explanation of material deprivation would have been helpful.

This paragraph starts off well, identifying the effect of low income on working conditions. There are two appropriate points about the lack of finance for materials for school work and school trips. However, the sentence about 'cultural capital' seems to misunderstand the meaning of the concept.

This shows weak interpretation of the term 'cultural differences', used in the Item with regard to social class. Here it is applied to ethnicity. The point made is somewhat dubious, in any case, and adds nothing to the answer.

A limited account, but some cultural differences in the home are mentioned and used briefly as evaluation.

The issue of higher education, mentioned in paragraph one, is returned to and developed in more detail. The point about family structure refers to family instability rather than material deprivation.

wish (or be forced) to earn a wage to help ease the family's money troubles, or may simply be discouraged from attending university by other low-income peers as it is 'not for them'.

Many sociologists (predominantly Marxist) believe that social class, and therefore lack of material wealth, affects educational achievement – after all, how can one study efficiently and effectively without a quiet place to work and the correct equipment? Similarly, the cost of things like transport, books, computers, uniform and sports equipment will be a problem for poor families. All of these are needed to help achievement. If poor children cannot go on school trips because of the expense, they may be bullied. Bourdieu spoke of the 'cultural capital' acquired by those with higher incomes, and thus lacking from the majority of low-income individuals.

However, Item A also cites 'cultural differences' as a reason for lack of educational achievement. For example, in Pakistani culture the woman's role is to be the housewife in a traditional nuclear family, and thus education has little part to play in her life: indeed practical qualities such as cooking and housekeeping are often prioritized. Similarly, boys may be expected to keep to traditional values and therefore may not feel that an education is important, instead viewing manual work as more desirable.

For some ethnic minority families language can also be a problem. However, Bernstein has shown that using restricted code language in any home can lead to difficulties at school. Parents' values and attitudes, and their own level of education, can also hold children back. Therefore, it's not just a matter of material differences.

Further, one's family structure may be important: those who live in a stable family are more likely to achieve well, whereas those with troubles at home tend to be emotionally drained and thus put little effort into their school work. As a consequence, this puts many off the idea of higher education, instead favouring an immediate job which allows them to become financially independent as quickly as possible. Similarly, dropout rates for poorer students are higher than for middle-class ones, and this is likely to increase with higher fees. Even when they are at school many children still have to work and therefore have less time for study.

Overall, it would seem that there is certainly evidence to suggest that material deprivation is the main factor in educational underachievement. As Bourdieu shows, those with a lack of income are often at a disadvantage right from the start of school, and interactionists would argue that many are labelled as potential troublemakers from the outset, perhaps leading to a sense of master status (where the children themselves believe they are 'bad'). And while there is evidence that socialization can play a role, the aspirations of wealthy upper-class boys would be very different from working-class ones. So social class is the most important reason for failure.

The first sentence makes a claim that has not been substantiated – the importance of other factors has not been discussed, so it's impossible to say that material deprivation is the 'main factor'.

However, the references to interactionist views and labelling do show potential evaluation. This could be developed, and the relationship between material deprivation and labelling could be explored. Similarly, the references to socialization and cultural differences suggest further points of evaluation – that these might be equally or even more important than material deprivation.

Overall, this answer makes a number of valid points, particularly where there is a clear focus on material deprivation. However, attempts to assess the importance of material deprivation are weak. Some appropriate sociological concepts are used and some of the factors are analysed.

Other aspects of material deprivation could be included, such as the effects of poor diet, ill health, poor housing, the need to work while at school, the area lived in and schools available.

This answer has insufficient evaluation for top marks. This could be provided by comparing the influence of material and cultural factors in the home; identifying differences of gender and ethnicity within social classes and/or contrasting home effects with in-school factors such as labelling.

Mark 13/20

Methods in Context

05 *Using material from **Item B** and elsewhere, assess the strengths and limitations of using participant observation for investigating teacher expectations of pupils' educational achievement.* **[20 marks]**

Participant observation is where a sociologist spends time with a particular group they are researching in order to study their behaviour. A sociologist can either be overt or covert in their participation. Educational achievement relates to a pupil's overall progress and success at school.

One advantage of using participant observation when studying teachers' expectations of pupils is that the researcher can see how the respondents act in their natural environment. For example the researcher can see how a teacher treats their students. This is a strength of participant observation because it is possible to see any teacher bias which may be lied about in other methods such as interviews. Another strength is that the researcher can see how a student responds. This may affect a student's achievement, for example bad behaviour often means poor achievement. This may also be lied about or hidden in other methods. Finally a researcher can measure the effect of the teacher's opinion. This means that a teacher's opinion of a student may affect their expectations also. ☞

A reasonable introduction, explaining terms, but with no reference to the main focus of the question.

A couple of strengths of participant observation are mentioned, and an attempt to link these to the question. However, the points could equally be applied to any research situation; they are not specific to this particular context. There is some drift to issues of achievement.

Several more strengths of participant observation are outlined, but the focus is still only on the method, not its application.

There is a weak attempt here to link with the particular issue, through a reference to the Item and the 'closed social setting' of the school However, this is not developed – there is little offered beyond a reference to a weakness that might occur in any participant observation research.

The conclusion brings together some of the points made and contrasts participant observation with other methods. However, there is no link to the question.

Participant observation is clearly a strength in this sense because the researcher is able to see the true picture of what goes on. Participant observation also has several other advantages, for example feminists like this type of method as it gives something back to the respondent. This is because a researcher is able to engage with their group, meaning that they are not just taking their information without giving something back to the people.

However participant observation also has several disadvantages. For example a school setting may be seen as a 'closed' social setting. This means that a sociologist may find it hard to engage with the group. This acts as a limitation because the sociologist will not be able to have a highly in-depth study. Additionally participant observation can have the negative effect of changing people's attitudes. For example when a person is watching a group, unless they are used to it, they will act differently. This is known as the Hawthorne effect. This also acts as a limitation as the study will not be valid or truthful. Realists are an example of one perspective that is critical of participant observation because they believe there is a need for quantitative research where trends and patterns can be recognized. This also acts as a limitation because a low level of reliability means that study cannot be repeated with the same results found.

In conclusion the strengths of participant observation highlight it as a very valid method to undertake and is approved by feminists. However there are also several limitations which may affect the level of quality. On the other hand there are other forms of method that may be seen as more suited to studying teacher expectations. For example interviewing may be seen as more suitable as it may be harder to lie, such as in unstructured interviews when the researcher can properly engage with a respondent. However quantitative data may be seen as better as trends and patterns can then be recognized.

Overall, this is a weak answer. There is insufficient focus on the question. The answer considers a number of strengths and weaknesses of the method, which is good, but these are not applied to the context of investigating teacher expectations. In some places there is a drift to discussion of the substantive area, rather than method. There is no mention of different theoretical perspectives, or of the difference between overt and covert observation.

It is essential that an answer to a methods in context question has a clear focus. The examination paper says very clearly that: 'you need to apply your knowledge and understanding of sociological research methods to the study of this particular issue in education.' To do this successfully the answer needs to go much further than a discussion of the method. It should include discussion of relevant research characteristics and how these might relate to the use of the method in question. For example, some of the following issues could be included:

- Observation in a classroom is likely to be overt. The characteristics of the classroom make it a closed social setting, and teachers may resent any intrusion into their classroom; they may see the intruder as a 'spy' sent by the head or Ofsted etc.☞

- The fact that teachers are used to being observed, and are therefore used to creating a good impression, means that they may be very careful about how they deal with pupils when there is an observer present.

- If the nature of the study is revealed, the teachers may ensure that all pupils are treated the same; if it is not revealed, this may lead to ethical issues.

- The pupils themselves may also react to being watched in the classroom. This may lead to very good behaviour that could hide what might normally be revealed in terms of evidence of teacher expectations.

- An additional place for observation could be the staffroom and/or teachers' meetings. There may be some possibility of covert observation here, as another member of staff or teaching assistant.

- In these situations it might be difficult to identify expectations without asking questions. There is no guarantee that expectations and attitudes towards different pupils would be revealed. It might also be difficult to record statements overheard, though the role of teacher might provide a good opportunity for writing notes.

Mark 8/20

Research Methods

06 *Explain what is meant by a 'representative sample'.* [**2 marks**]

A representative sample is a group of researched people or data whose results can be applied to represent their entire subculture or population. For example, if you interview 60 000 British men about their views on homophobia you could apply this to the British population as a whole.

The notion of a sample is explained appropriately. However, to explain the notion of 'representative', the answer needs to show that it is a cross-section typical of the wider group. This is not done here.

Mark 1/2

07 *Suggest **two** reasons why a researcher may choose to use structured rather than unstructured interviews.* [**4 marks**]

One reason why a researcher may use structured interviews rather than unstructured ones is to gain statistical (or quantitative) data that can be pre-coded.

Secondly, using this research method allows the researcher to carry out a study high in objectivity (due to the researcher not having much interaction with the participant, thus lessening the chance of researcher bias).

Two appropriate reasons are given.

Other possible answers might include: higher reliability (replicability); more representative; quicker to conduct; less training needed.

Mark 4/4

08 *Identify **two** practical reasons for using postal questionnaires.* **[4 marks]**

Five appropriate answers are provided here: they are easy; cheap; can access many people; no need to employ staff; wide distribution; representativeness. The question only asked for two, though it may sometimes be useful to add an extra suggestion if you are not sure.

Other possible answers might be: no need for training; easy to quantify.

Mark 4/4

One practical reason for using postal questionnaires is that they are easy and cheap to do. This is because they can be sent out to lots of people at once which makes it easier than hand delivery. It also means that people do not need to be employed in order to send them out, therefore saving money. Another practical reason is that the questionnaires can be distributed widely. This means that representativeness is increased as it is sent to a lot of people who are distributed all over the country.

09 *Assess the usefulness of different forms of qualitative secondary sources in sociological research.* **[20 marks]**

A useful first paragraph, explaining the terms in the question and suggesting that 'usefulness' will be considered.

The term 'secondary sources' covers lots of material, from statistics collected by organizations and governments to personal diaries. All of these are produced by other people or organizations, but may be used by sociologists in their research. 'Qualitative sources' usually refers to the different types of documents that are available. These are more in-depth than the statistics and include letters, diaries and historical documents. Many of these sources are freely available, so this is an inexpensive way to research. They are all useful, but all of them also have their own problems which it is important to consider.

The strengths and weaknesses of diaries and letters are summarized, and appropriate examples are provided to illustrate these.

Diaries and letters can be useful forms of secondary data. The writers may be dead, so the sociologists can't actually interview them, but they are likely to be very valid, potentially providing reasons for why people did certain things at the time: for example, Anne Frank's diary shows the fear felt by Jews. It's possible to get a real insight into people's feelings. However, the writers can be very biased, trying to show themselves to be good and not telling the whole truth, which sometimes makes diaries and letters less valid as they're very subjective. The 'Polish Peasant' study by Thomas and Zaniecki used letters sent between Poland and America, but found that the young migrants often didn't tell the folks back home what they were really doing.

Two perspectives are used to contrast sociological views on these methods, and a further evaluative point is made. An opportunity is missed to link to the concept of representativeness.

Interpretivist sociologists use these forms of documents because of the depth of information and they are seen as authentic. They can be very rich and detailed. However, positivists don't use them because they are seen as unreliable and depend on the way the researcher interprets them. In the past, most diaries and letters were only written by the wealthy, so they are limited in what they can tell us about ordinary people.

Content of the media can also be very useful for sociologists as a form of secondary data. The increasing use of the internet, along with television ☞

and radio programmes, has meant that there are lots of resources that sociologists can easily use. This is usually done by content analysis. This is when newspaper articles, adverts or TV programmes are analysed for their content, to see how things are portrayed; for example female or disabled stereotypes. This is a cheap source of information and can be qualitative or quantitative, such as the study of gender roles in children's books by Lobban. The internet is a good source, but there are lots of articles which aren't true.

One last type of qualitative secondary source is novels and autobiographies. Like the diaries and letters, these may give great insight into how people feel about events or situations. With any of these sources, sociologists have to remember that people may be writing for their own reasons and as a result, sociologists should always be careful to consider these things, and weigh up how valid they really are.

A number of evaluative points are made about another source – content analysis – and the variety of forms of data available. The account tends to be listy, with little analysis.

A brief account of novels and autobiographies, followed by a brief but sound conclusion.

This is a reasonably good answer. Both practical and theoretical issues are considered, though ethics is not mentioned. A good range of qualitative sources are covered and examples are provided for several of these. The question is interpreted well and a range of appropriate material is applied. There is some evidence of the skills of analysis and evaluation. Sociological concepts are used.

However, there are a number of ways in which this answer could be improved to reach top marks. A number of opportunities are lost to focus on the key concepts of representativeness, reliability and validity. These need to be explained and appropriate links made to the different sources.

The final examples of novels and autobiographies are not explained. It would be useful to analyse the main strengths and weaknesses of these methods, such as: novels are fiction, so untrue, but do provide insight; autobiographies consist of a person's own account, but can't be relied upon for truthfulness. Other sources such as historical and public documents could be included to increase the range.

The discussion about theoretical perspectives in paragraph three could include a link to Marxist and feminist views, showing how these perspectives see the ruling class and men as dominating these sources.
Mark: 13/20

Total marks: 1 + 4 + 7 + 13 + 8 + 1 + 4 + 4 + 13 = 55/90 = Grade C

The following examples show how you can improve your answers to the short questions for Education with Research Methods.

01 *Explain what is meant by the term 'longitudinal study'.* **[2 marks]**

All studies take place over a period of time. The particular characteristics of this type of study are not identified.
Mark 0/2

Weak answer

A study done for a period of time.

Some knowledge is shown but there is no reference to the sample studied – this could be a series of different samples
Mark 1/2

Better answer

A study carried out over a long period of time.

The term has been explained correctly
Mark 2/2

Good answer

Studying the same sample of people at intervals over a period of time.

02 *Suggest **three** possible effects on pupils of being placed in lower sets.* **[6 marks]**

The first sentence is about the development of a subculture but does not indicate two different effects, so 2 marks. The second is too vague.
Mark 2/6

Weak answer

Pupils will join a subculture and will be affected by their peer group.

They will miss their friends.

Two appropriate answers are given. The final answer is insufficient, though it hints at the fact that it may be difficult to move up again. 1 mark for a partial answer.
Mark 5/6

Better answer

When they are put in a lower set, pupils may join an anti-school subculture.

The teachers will not have as much time for them.

They will be stuck.

Three effects explained clearly. Other suitable answers might include: teachers may lower their expectations; pupils may lose self-esteem and confidence; less may be learnt because of disruptive behaviour.
Mark 6/6

Good answer

Once you are in a lower set, you will work more slowly, so it's difficult to get back up to a higher set.

A subculture may form that is anti schoolwork, so achievement will be less.

The lower set might have less capable teachers, who are not the best for that subject.

Education and Research Methods

Academies	Schools that are independent of local authority control, set up by the Labour government of 1997 to 2010 in inner-cities, and schools that opted out of local authority control under the coalition government from 2010
Accuracy	Whether the author of a **document** has the knowledge to provide a true record of something
Achieved status	A position in society, which affects the way others view you that is earned, at least partly, through your own efforts, e.g. a job
Alienation	A sense of being distanced from something so that it feels alien, e.g. feeling a lack of connection and fulfilment in work
Anti-school subcultures	**Subcultures** opposed to the **dominant values** of a school
Ascribed status	A position in society, which affects the way others view you that is given by birth, e.g. being male or female
Attitudes survey	A **survey** collecting information about subjective opinions
Authenticity	How genuine **documents** are
Authorship	Whether a **document** was written by the author to whom it is attributed
Availability	Whether **documents** have survived and are accessible to researchers
Bands/banding	The placing of pupils into broad groups according to their general academic ability
Bourgeoisie	The **ruling class** in **capitalism** who own property such as **capital**, businesses and shares
Breadwinner	The person in a household who does the most paid work
Capital	Assets, which can be used to produce more resources
Capitalist society/ capitalism	A society in which people are employed for wages, and businesses are set up with the aim of making a profit
Catchment area	The geographical area from which pupils eligible to attend the school are drawn
Causal relationship	When one thing leads to another thing happening
Case study	An individual example of something that is studied in depth
Census	A **social survey** carried out by the government every 10 years in the UK, collecting standardized data about the whole of the population
Choice	The idea that parents should be able to choose which institution their children go to for their education
City Technology College	New schools set up in inner-cities with an emphasis on scientific and technical subjects along with maths. Independent of **LEAs** and partly funded by businesses
Class/social class	Groups within society distinguished by their economic position and who are therefore unequal, e.g. the **middle class** in better paid, non-manual jobs and the **working class** in less well-paid, physical jobs
Class subculture	The distinctive lifestyle associated with a particular **class**
Collaborative interviewing	Interviewing in which the interviewees become full partners in the research

Collectivist	Putting the interests of the social group before the interests of the individual
Compensatory education	Additional education provided to try to address underperformance by particular social groups in the education system
Competition	When individuals or businesses try to do better than one another, e.g., in selling more goods than another company
Complementarity	Where different methods are combined to dovetail different aspects of an investigation
Comprehensive school	A type of school attended by all children regardless of ability or aptitude
Confidentiality	Keeping data about specific individuals secret
Conflict theory	Theory of society, which sees one or more groups in competition for scarce or valued goods, examples include Marxism and **feminism**
Content analysis	Research in which the content of the mass media is analysed
Control group	In an **experiment**, a group in which **variables** are not changed so that the effects of changing one variable in another group can be determined
Correlation	A statistical tendency for two things to be found together
Correspondence principle	In the **Marxist** theory of Bowles and Gintis, the idea that the structure, organization and values of educational institutions reflect, or correspond to, the structure organization and values of the workplace in **capitalist** businesses
Counterculture	The beliefs and lifestyle of a group who are opposed to the dominant culture
Counter-school culture	The beliefs of a group who are opposed to the **values** of those in authority at a school
Covert participant observation	**Participant observation** where the researcher does not reveal that they are conducting research to the people being observed
Cream-skimming	Schools or other educational institutions selecting the most able pupils/students to attend their institution
Credibility	How believable a **document** is
Crisis in masculinity	The idea that clear roles for men in society no longer exist as a result of the decline in male-dominated manual work or changes in society's **culture**
Cultural capital	Non-material assets such as classical knowledge and lifestyle, which are valued by society and can be helpful in achieving educational success
Cultural deprivation	Lacking or being deficient in the attitudes, **values**, knowledge, linguistic ability or lifestyles necessary to succeed in the education system
Cultural factors	Factors concerned with lifestyle, attitudes and values, which might affect achievement in education, as opposed to **material factors**
Culture	The **norms**, **values**, attitudes and lifestyle of a social group
Curriculum	The formal content of what is taught in schools and other educational institutions
Deferred gratification	Putting off pleasure now in order to achieve greater pleasure in the future, e.g. saving for a deposit on a house
Deterministic	A theory, which sees behaviour as entirely determined by external circumstances, leaving the individual with little or no choice about how they behave

Deviants	People who do not abide by the norms of society
Differential educational achievement	Systematic differences in the performance of social groups in the education system, e.g. between **social classes**
Disconnected choosers	Parents who lack the skills and resources to exercise **choice** effectively in the education system
Division of labour	The way in which jobs are divided up between two or more people, e.g. who does particular tasks in a household
Documents	Any physical artefacts containing information that could be used by sociologists as a source of data
Dominant culture	The **culture** that is most powerful and has the highest status in a society
Economic base	In Marxist theory, the foundation of society consisting of the economic system
Economic capital	Material assets such as housing and income, which can be helpful in achieving educational success
Education Action Zones	Areas of deprived inner-cities where additional **compensatory education** schemes were started in the 1970s
Educational triage	The rationing of education so that only those who are likely to attain targets through receiving extra help are provided with additional assistance
Efficiency	Achieving the best possible outcomes using the least possible resources
Egoism	According to Durkheim, a situation where people are not well integrated into social groups and therefore are mainly concerned with themselves rather than others
Elaborated codes	A type of speech where the meanings are filled in and made explicit, sentences tend to be longer and more complex than in **restricted codes**
Equality of opportunity	When every individual has an equal chance of success based upon their own ability and effort. Will tend to lead to inequality of outcome, i.e. some people will be more successful than others because they are more able or they work harder
Ethical factors	Factors concerned with morality
Ethnic group	A group within a population regarded by themselves or by others as culturally distinctive – they usually see themselves as having a common origin
Ethnographic study	The study of the lifestyle of a group of people
Experiment	An artificial situation set up by a researcher in order to test a **hypothesis**
Explanatory survey	A **survey** testing theories or **hypotheses**
External rewards	Things that are given to someone in recognition of their efforts, e.g. wages or exam certificates – this contrast to internal rewards such as personal satisfaction or happiness
Facilitation	Where one method is used to assist or develop use of another method
Factual survey	A **survey** collecting descriptive information
Falsify/falsification	Proving something wrong
Fatalism	A belief that your chances in life are shaped by luck or fate rather than feeling you can determine them by you own efforts
Femininity	The social roles and behaviour expected of women in a particular **culture**

Feminism	Theory of society, which claims that women are disadvantaged and exploited by men, while men are dominant and run society in their own interests
Field experiments	An **experiment** conducted in a natural social setting rather them in a laboratory
Fixed-choice questions	Questions where respondent has to choose from a range of predetermined responses
Focus group	A group interview used to collect data on opinions and attitudes
Formal content analysis	Analysis of mass media content in which numerical data is produced about the frequency of different types of content appearing in a source
Formal curriculum	The official content (subject and courses) of educational institutions
Fragmented	Divided into small pieces so that no coherent whole exists
Free market	A system in which businesses can compete with one another without state interference
Free schools	Schools set up by charities, teachers, businesses or parents but funded by the **state**, they were introduced by the coalition government after 2010
Functionalism	A sociological perspective, which believes that social institutions serve some positive purpose
Functionally important jobs	Occupations, which are believed to play a particularly crucial role in the effective functioning of society
Future-time orientation	Think ahead rather than living in the moment
Functions	Useful jobs performed by an institution for society
Gender gap	The difference in the achievement of males and females in the education system
Gender roles	The socially expected behaviour of men and women in a particular society
Gender socialization	The way in which males and females are taught to behave differently in a particular society
Generalizability	How reasonable it is to make statements about a wider **population** on the basis of a particular **sample**
Grammar schools	Secondary schools in which admission is granted on the basis of ability – originally measured through an IQ test, the 11+
Grant-maintained schools	Schools funded directly by government, independent of Local Education Authorities (LEAs)
Group interview	An **interview** where several interviewees are questioned together
Habitus	The dispositions, tastes and lifestyles associated with a particular **social class**
Hawthorne effect	When people being observed in observational research or an **experiment** change their behaviour because they are aware that they are being monitored
Hegemony/ hegemonic	Political or cultural dominance
Hidden curriculum	The hidden, informal messages and lessons outside the formal curriculum that come from the way schooling is organized
Hierarchy	Where individuals are ranked above and below one another, and orders and instructions flow from the top of the hierarchy towards the bottom

Hypothesis	A statement to be tested through research
Ideal pupil	The image held by teachers of the sort of pupil they would choose to have in their classes if they were allowed to select those whom they taught
Ideology	A distorted set of beliefs, which favour the interests of a particular social group
Immediate gratification	Enjoying yourself now, e.g. spending your wage packet as soon as you get it
Income	Money being received by an individual or social group
Individual achievement	When each person is primarily concerned for their own success rather than the success of a social group as a whole
Individualism	An emphasis upon the desires or interests of individual people rather than those of wider social groups
Industrialization	The process whereby manufacturing takes over from agriculture as the most important component in a society's economy
Industrial society	A society that has undergone the process of **industrialization**
Inequality of opportunity	When some individuals or groups have more chance of success than others because of unfair advantages and disadvantages
Informed consent	Agreeing to take part in research while fully aware of the purpose of the research and its implications
Infrastructure	In Marxist theory, the foundation of society consisting of the economic system (same as **economic base**)
Institutional racism	'The collective failure of an organization to provide an appropriate and professional service to people because of their colour, culture, or ethnic origin' (MacPherson, 1999)
Interactionism	An interpretivist sociological perspective, which emphasizes **meanings**, **motives** and **self-concepts**
Interpretative understanding	Being able to understand what a **document** signifies
Interview	A research method in which one or more people ask an individual or group a series of questions
Interviewer bias	When the results of interviews are distorted by the presence or behaviour of the interviewer
IQ test	An intelligence test designed to test a person's abstract reasoning ability rather than their knowledge of subjects
Key informant	A respondent or interviewee who is particularly helpful to a researcher
Label/labelling	The qualities or the identity conferred on a person or social group through the expressed opinions of others
Labour market	The overall structure of the market in which employers and workers buy and sell labour
Laws	Statements about universal relationships of cause and effect
League tables	Tables ranking schools in terms of their performance in exams or by other criteria

LEAs	Local Education Authorities responsible for running most aspects of the education system in a particular area
Left wing	Political views, which tend to favour greater equality through the redistribution of wealth and income from rich to poor, and which offer strong support for state intervention in the economy
Legitimate	Used as a verb – to make something seem fair and reasonable. Used as a noun – something, which is accepted as fair and reasonable
Liberal feminism	A version of **feminism**, which is relatively moderate and believes that the position of women in society can be improved through reform rather than radical or revolutionary change
Life course	The development and change in people's lives over periods of time, unlike life-cycle the life course does not have fixed and predictable stages
Life documents	Private documents created by individuals, used to record subjective thoughts and feelings
Life history	An in-depth study of an individual person's life
Literal understanding	Being able to read, decipher or translate the content of a **document**
Longitudinal study	A study that takes place over an extended period of time often with periodic gathering of data
Manual labour/ manual jobs	Work, which primarily involves physical efforts rather than thought
Marketization	Introducing **competition** into education along with **formula funding** so that educational institutions start to act like businesses
Market liberal	Another term for the **New Right** who believe in the **free-market**
Marxist	Person following the theory of Karl Marx, which argues that societies are dominated by a **ruling class**, which owns the **means of production**
Masculinity	The behaviour and social roles expected of men in a particular culture
Material factors	Factors to do with money and other material resources (e.g. housing), which might affect performance in education, as opposed to **cultural factors**
Material resources	Physical and financial possessions, which can be useful in achieving objectives such as success in education
Meanings	The interpretations made by people of acts, words or other symbols, in the context of evaluating **documents**
Means of production	Those things required to produce goods such as land machinery, capital, technical knowledge and workers
Merit	Worth judged in terms of ability and effort
Meritocracy/ meritocratic society	A society in which people's positions, e.g. their jobs, are determined on merit, i.e. according to their abilities and how hard they have worked
Methodology	The methods used to collect data and the philosophy underlying the production of sociological data
Middle class	People who have white-collar jobs that require some qualifications and are generally better paid than the **working class**

Migration	The movements of people between different geographical areas
Mixed ability	A class where all pupils are taught together regardless of their level of ability
Mode of production	A system of producing things, which dominates society, e.g. capitalism
Moral panic	A sudden and illogical outburst of public concern about some perceived decline in the moral standards of society, the implication is that the concern is exaggerated or does not match reality
Motives	The subjective reasons for behaving in particular ways
Multicultural curriculum	A **curriculum** that reflects the lifestyles (e.g. religions), history and interests of pupils/students from different **ethnic groups**
Multi-stage sampling	Sampling in which a sample of a sample is taken, e.g. a sample of voters in a sample of constituencies
National Curriculum	Subjects and subject content laid down by central government, which it is compulsory for schools to teach. First introduced in 1988
Neo-liberal	Another term for the **New Right** who believe in the **free-market**
Neo-Marxism	New versions of Marxism, which are strongly influenced by the works of Karl Marx but disagree with some aspects of them and have been updated to fit contemporary society
New Labour	The Labour Party under the leadership of Tony Blair and Gordon Brown, which distanced itself from previous **social democratic** policies and instead adopted the **Third Way**
New Right	Politicians, thinkers and writers who support the free-market rather than state intervention and who believe that traditional moral values should be preserved
Non-directive interviewing	Interviewing in which the interviewer does not reveal their own opinions or suggest answers to the respondents
Non-manual labour	Work that does not primarily require physical effort, e.g. office work
Non-representative sampling	A sampling technique in which people who are not typical of a wider **population** are chosen
Norms	Specific, informal rules of behaviour in a particular society
Objectivity	Making truthful statements about the world, which are not influenced by personal opinion or preferences
Observation	A research method in which one or more researchers watch individuals or social groups and record some data
Occupational groups	Clusters of similar jobs, e.g. professional or **service sector** jobs. Occupational groups are sometimes used as a way of distinguishing **social classes**
Official statistics	Numerical data produced by government agencies
Open-ended questions	Questions where the respondents may give whatever response they think fit and do not have to choose from pre-determined options
Operationalizing	Defining a concept in a form that can be measured, usually by identifying a series of indicators
Opportunity sampling	Sampling in which people are chosen happen to be easily accessible and willing to participate in the research

Oversubscribed school	A school that more pupils wish to attend than there are places available
Overt participant observation	**Participant observation** where the researcher is open about the fact that they are conducting research
Panel study	A **longitudinal study**, used to collect data from a sample of people over a number of years
Participant observation	Research conducted by observing a group while taking part in its activities
Particularistic standards	When people are judged as particular individuals, e.g. parents judging children
Partly structured interviews	An interview in which there are a small number of preset questions or list of topics that need to be covered
Patriarchy	Literally 'rule by the father', usually used by **feminists** to refer to a system in which men have more **power** than women and shape how societies run
Peer group	A group of people with a similar **status**, and often age, to whom you compare yourself and who may exercise influence on your behaviour
Pilot study	A preliminary small-scale trial study carried out before the main research in order to test the feasibility of the main study and to refine the research methods being used
Population	The total group the sociologist is interested in when conducting research
Positivism	A philosophy of social research based upon scientific ideas of **objectivity**
Poverty	Lacking the resources to pay for the minimum acceptable lifestyle
Power	The ability of a person to get their own way or to determine outcomes regardless of the wishes of others
Practical factor/ issue	A factor in research to do with time, money or access as opposed to **ethical** or **theoretical issues**
Pre-industrial society	Societies that existed before industrialization where most production was based upon agriculture
Private documents	**Documents** produced by individuals, which are not normally available for members of the public to access
Privileged/skilled choosers	Parents who have the resources and skills necessary to be able to make effective choices in the education system
Present-time orientation	Living life in the moment rather than worrying about the future
Primary data source	Data collected by sociologists themselves
Primary socialization	The first stage of the process through which children learn the culture of their society, it takes place in the family
Private enterprise	**Businesses** owned by individuals or shareholders and run in order to make a profit
Private schools	Schools run by non-state organizations where pupils have to pay to attend
Progressive taxation	A taxation policy designed to reduce inequality in society by taking more tax from those on high incomes than those on low incomes
Public documents	**Documents** that are readily available for members of the public to access

Public schools	High status and expensive **private schools** in Britain
Qualitative data	Data that takes a non-numerical form, e.g. words and images
Quantitative data	Data that takes a numerical form
Questionnaire	A written list of questions
Quota sampling	A system in which quotas are established, which determine how many people with particular characteristics are studied. Once a quota is filled no more people in that category are included
Racism	Discriminatory beliefs or actions based upon a person's supposed 'race' or ethnic group
Random sampling	A system in which every sampling unit has an equal chance of being chosen, e.g. drawn out of a hat
Relative autonomy	In Marxist theory, a degree of independence – particularly when parts of the **superstructure** have some independence from the **economic base** and the **ruling class**
Reliability	Data is reliable if another researcher using identical methods would produce the same results
Representativeness	How typical data is of a wider **population**
Replication	Producing a copy of something – particularly repeating research to check results
Response-rate	The proportion of selected subjects who take go on to part in research, e.g. by returning a **questionnaire**
Restricted codes	A type of shorthand speech where meanings are not made fully explicit – it uses short, simple and often unfinished sentences
Right wing	Political views that tend to favour **free-markets** over state intervention, support **competition**, and therefore believe that inequality is an inevitable part of society
Role allocation	Determining which individuals carry out which roles, e.g. deciding who does what jobs
Ruling class	In Marxist theory, the group who are dominant in society by virtue of their wealth and power
Sample	A group selected from within a wider **population** with whom research is carried out
Sampling frame	A list of individual **sampling units** from which a **sample** is drawn
Sampling unit	The individual person or thing that is the subject of research and is selected to be part of a **sample** from a **population**
Secondary data/ source	Existing data used by a sociologists rather than data derived from research
Secondary modern school	Schools attended by students who had failed to get into selective **grammar schools**. Focus on vocational, rather than academic, education
Selective schools	Schools that can choose some or all of their pupils on the basis of ability, or some other criteria
Self-concept	The way a person sees or defines themselves
Self-fulfilling prophecy	Something that occurs because somebody has predicted that it will happen

Semi-structured interviews	Type of interview that combines open and fixed-choice questions and/or where the structure gives the interviewer flexibility in choice and wording of questions
Service sector	Parts of the economy involved in providing services to people rather than manufacturing
Set/setting	The placement of pupils in groups according to their ability in a particular subject
Sexism	Discriminatory beliefs or actions based upon a person's sex
Sex stereotyping	Treating males and females according to widely held **stereotypes** of typical behaviour
Shop-floor culture	The attitudes and behaviour of workers in factories and similar places of work, particularly behaviour by men
Sincerity	Whether the author of a **document** intends to provide a true account or to mislead their readers
Sites of ideological struggle	A location where competing belief systems are held by individuals struggling to achieve dominance, e.g. schools where different factors have different **values**
Snowballing	A sampling technique in which a member of a sample puts the researcher in touch with other potential members for the sample
Social capital	The possession of valuable social contacts, which can assist in achieving success in education
Social construction	A behaviour or practice, which is produced by society even though it may seem natural or biological
Social democrat	A political viewpoint associated with the traditional Labour Party, which believes in creating greater equality through reforms of **capitalist** society. Associated with the introduction of **comprehensives schools**
Social facts	Truthful statements about social phenomena
Social mobility	The movement of people between social groups, especially social classes
Social solidarity	A sense of belonging, commitment and loyalty to a social group
Socialization	The process through which people learn the culture of their society
Soundness	Whether a **document** is complete and is **reliable**
State	The practices and institutions directly or indirectly controlled by the government and its bureaucracy in a country
Status	The amount of esteem in which people are held by others in society
Stereotype	A simplified and usually highly misleading image of a social group
Stratified random sampling	A system of sampling in which the population is divided into groups according to important **variables** such as **class**, gender and **ethnicity,** and the sample is then chosen in the same proportions as their preponderance in the population
Streams/streaming	The placing of pupils in groups according to their general academic ability
Structured interview	An interview in which questions are pre-determined
Subculture	A group within a wider culture, which has significantly different **norms**, attitudes, **values** and lifestyle to other groups in society, while sharing some aspects of the wider culture
Subject class	In Marxist theory, the group in society who are dominated by the **ruling class** whom they have to work for because they lack the property to produce goods for themselves. The subject class are exploited by the **ruling class**

Superstructure	In Marxist theory, the non-economic parts of society such as the family, which are shaped by the economy and controlled by the **ruling class**
Sure Start	Schemes to provide additional pre-school education and extra educational resources, including help for parents, in deprived, inner-city areas
Surplus value	Profits made by the ruling class
Survey	Research collecting standardized information about a large group of people
Survival	Whether **documents** still exist or not
Symbolic capital	Possession of high social status, e.g. that which comes from having an image of respectability
Technical schools	Schools for those believed to have technical talents set up as part of the **tripartite system**
Textual analysis	The detailed analysis of small pieces of text in the mass media
Thematic analysis	Analysis of the mass media in which the underlying message of the coverage of a particular topic is interpreted
Theoretical factors	Factors concerned with the quality of information produced in research
Third Way	The philosophy of the '**New Labour**' Party, which claims to steer a middle way between **left-wing** and **right-wing** politics
Triangulation	The use of several different research methods in one study
Tripartite system	The system of secondary **state** education set up in Britain in 1944 in which children went to one of three types of school – **grammar**, **secondary modern** or **technical**
Typology	A classification of different types of a phenomenon
Underachievement	Doing less well than your potential suggests you should do in the education system
Universal	Found in all societies
Universalistic standards	When people are judged according to an abstract set of standards, e.g. when exams are being marked
Unstructured interview	An interview in which there are no or very few predetermined questions
Upper class	The highest **social class** in society consisting of those who own wealth or property
Upward social mobility	Moving from one **social class** to a higher **class**
Values	General beliefs about what is right or wrong in a particular society
Validity	How true data is, i.e. how close the fit is between the data and reality
Variable	A cause or an effect, something that can produce a change or can be changed
Vocational	Related to jobs, i.e. education designed to provide the skills necessary for work
Wealth	Money or saleable possessions possessed by an individual social group
Within-class groupings	Teaching where pupils are divided into different ability groups in the same classroom
Working class	People who do manual jobs, which require relatively few qualifications and are usually less well-paid than **middle-class** jobs
Youth culture	A **subculture** associated with a group of young people, particularly those associated with particular ways of dressing or musical tastes